Mouth Organ for Everyone

Learn Chromatic Harmonica – Beginners to Advanced Level

Author: *Riddhi Sanyal*
Editor: *Priyanka Sanyal*

Volume One | Self Publication

This book contains step by step guidelines on how to play Chromatic Harmonica. The content will help the learner to do self-learning and play independently.

Book has around 40 notations containing

- 10 Prelims
- 10 Beginners
- 10 Intermediate
- 10 Advanced

Songs & Tunes are on various genre like **children Music, Bollywood songs, Jazz, rhythmic, Folk, pop, Indian folk, waltz, Romantic, Soft Rock, classical, Christmas songs, marching** and so on;

Notation given in 3 ways - **Harmonica Tabs, Staff notes and Indian Swar**.

Paperback B/W at INDIA: Available at Amazon & Notion Press: ISBN: 9798889239390
EBook and Paperback Color: Available at Amazon all marketplaces / countries

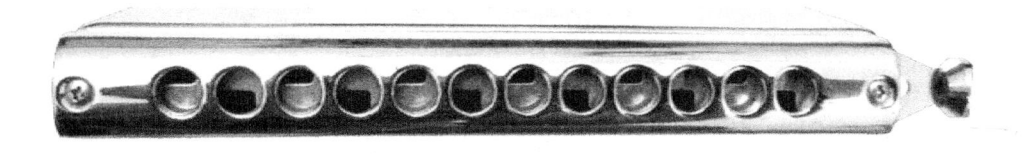

Mouth Organ For Everyone

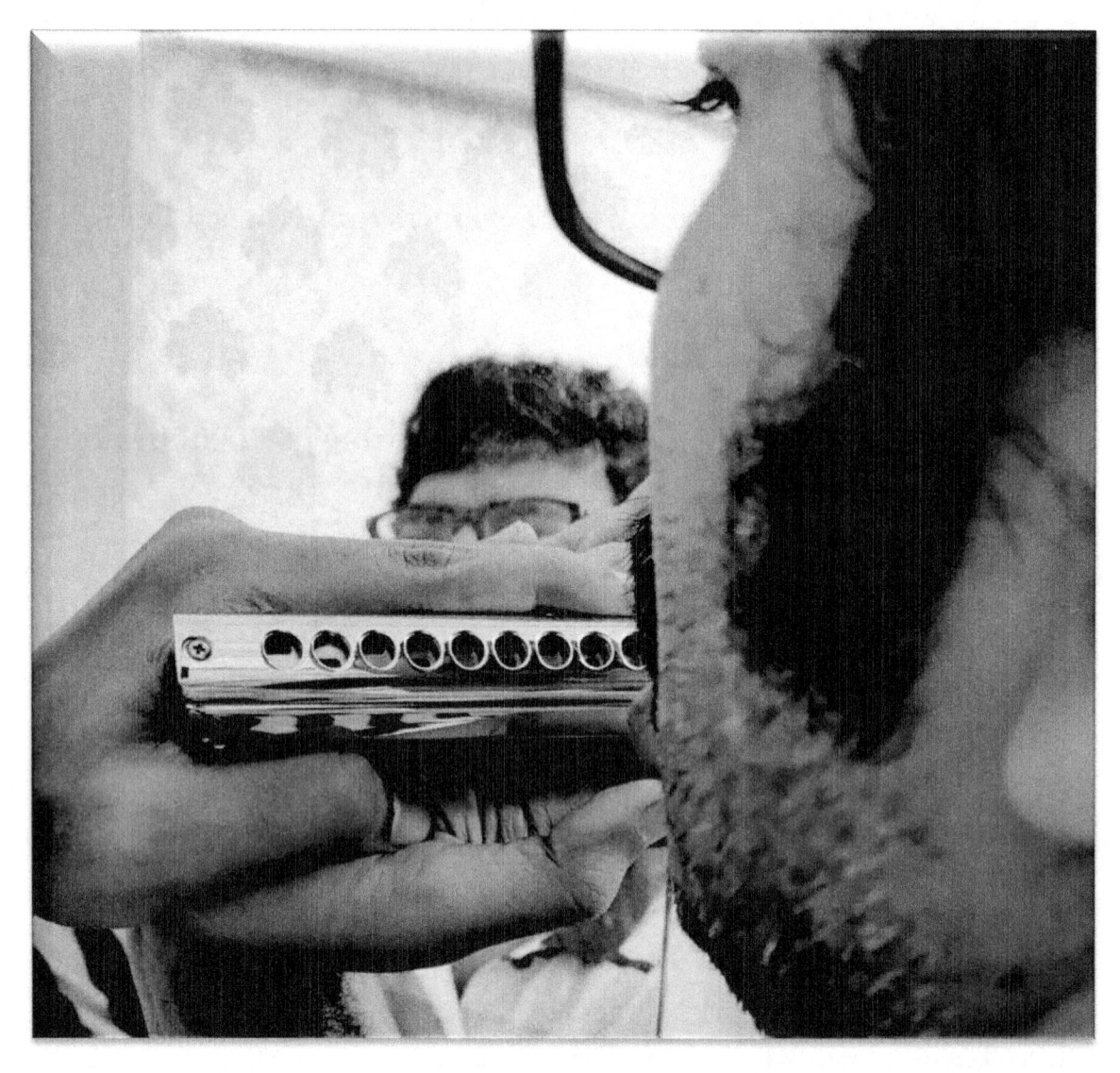

Figure 1: Author playing Harmonica in front of mirror to show the holding style

Mouth Organ For Everyone, Copyright ©2024, India, by Riddhi Sanyal. All Rights Reserved. No part of this book shall be reproduced in any manner whatsoever without written permission from the author, except in the case of brief quotations embodied in articles & reviews.

Table of Contents

1.0 Dedication 6
2.0 Preface 6
   2.1 Who can Read this book 6
   2.2 What makes this book different and unique from others 6
   2.3 Time to achieve the milestones 7
   2.4 About the Notations 7
3.0 Introduction to Harmonica 8
   3.1 Why this can be your choice of instrument 8
   3.2 How many sounds in a position 8
   3.3 Full of Harmony 9
   3.4 Types of Harmonica & Purposes 10
      3.4.1 Diatonic Harmonica: 10
      3.4.2 Chromatic Harmonica 11
      3.4.3 Tremolo Harmonica 13
   3.5 Style of Playing, Special Effects 15
      3.5.1 Holding Technique – 15
      3.5.2 Whistle Style: 16
      3.5.3 Tongue Assist Style: 17
      3.5.4 Special Effects: Vibrato 17
      3.5.5 Special Effects: Bending 17
   3.6 Which model to buy (for Beginner) 18
   3.7 Small tips to take care of your harmonica 19
4.0 Notations Conventions 20
   4.1 About the Middle C and Octaves: 20
   4.2 The Most Played Major Notes 23
   4.3 Staff Note symbols to remember 24
      4.3.1 Clef & Staff Lines: 24
      4.3.2 The Key Signature: 25
      4.3.3 Time Signature: 25
      4.3.4 The Measure 26
      4.3.5 The Note Symbols & Gaps 26
      4.3.6 The Tempo: 27

4.3.7	The Dotted Note or Augmentation Dot	27
4.3.8	Repeats	27
4.3.9	Further readings are listed as Reference:	29

5.0 Preliminary lessons for Harmonica 30

5.1	Learn the Octaves and play the middle OCTAVE	30
5.2	Play two same notes at a Time	32
5.3	Two sequential notes pattern	33
5.4	Play a pattern with skipping one note	35
5.5	Play simple notes to evolve into a Rhythm	36
5.6	Play three notes pattern	36
5.7	Four Notes pattern	37
5.8	Learn to play with Gaps	38
5.9	Have more control on Quarter & Eighth Notes with Gaps	40
5.10	Further Practices:	40

6.0 Beginners Tunes and Songs on Harmonica 42

6.1	Twinkle Twinkle Little Star	44
6.2	Wheels on the bus go round and round	45
6.3	Happy Birthday Tune	47
6.4	Row Row Row Your Boat	49
6.5	Old MacDonald had a Farm – the famous Rhythmic tune	51
6.6	We Shall Overcome	53
6.7	Jingle Bells	55
6.8	Do-A-Deer – The tune from Sound of Music	57
6.9	Sholay – Harmonica Theme Tune	59
6.10	Simple Tune on *Deshkar* – by Guruji Sri D Madhusudan	60
6.11	Further Learning	62

7.0 Intermediate Level Tunes for Harmonica 65

7.1	A Chal Ke Tujhe	66
7.2	Santa Lucia	70
7.3	Jamaica Farewell	72
7.4	Title Music – by Sri D. Madhusudan	74
7.5	"O Sona Byang O Kola Byang" - Gems from Legend Salil Chowdhury	76

7.6	Hai Aapna Dil	78
7.7	Minuet – Gems from Bach	81
7.8	Pran Chay Chokkhu Na Chay – A Rhythmic Song from Gurudev Sri Rabindranath Tagore	83
7.9	Five Hundred Miles – Famous tune for Harmonica	86
7.10	Music for Wind – Created by Guruji Sri D. Madhusudan	88
7.11	Further Learning	91
8.0	Advance Level Songs / Tunes for Harmonica	93
8.1	The Lion King Song	95
8.2	March Music – Composed by Sri D. Madhusudan	99
8.3	Chala Jata Hoon	102
8.4	Indian Folk Music – Tomay Hrid Majhare Rakhbo	106
8.5	Waltz 12 By D. Madhusudan – 12 Notes Practice	108
8.6	Surero Ei Jhor Jhor Jhorna – Learn Rhythm from Salil Chowdhury's song	112
8.7	Yeh Dosti Hum Nahi Todenge	116
8.8	Ajeeb Dastan Hai Yeh	120
8.9	Salute to Covid Warriors – By Sri D. Madhusudan	124
8.10	Mere Sapno Ki Rani Kab Aayegi Tu	127
8.11	Further Learning	132
9.0	Index, References & Appendix:	135
9.1	Index of Figures, Tables, Note Symbols & Lessons:	135
9.2	References	136
9.3	Appendix	138
10.0	About The Author	140
11.0	Other Publications from the Author	141
12.0	Feedback & Contacts	142

Author Page: https://www.amazon.com/author/riddhi (you can get all published books here in this link) ... 142

Email: Riddhi.Sanyal@gmail.com ... 142

Whatsapp Number: +91 9051653871 ... 142

YouTube Channel: https://www.youtube.com/c/MusicalJourneys ... 142

Facebook Page: https://www.facebook.com/mu.instr ... 142

Instagram: https://www.instagram.com/riddhi.sanyal/ ... 142

1.0 Dedication

- Gurudeb Swami Sadhanananda Giri Maharaj
- Musical Maestro, Guruji Sri Madhusudan Das
- MAA, BABA, Priyanka, Pragyan and all family members to bless & support me in music
- All friends who supports me

2.0 Preface

This book was in my mind since a long time ago. Everything has a proper time to start and so this one too. The primary objective of this book is to make the quality lessons for anyone who wants to learn Harmonica.

2.1 Who can Read this book

- Beginners in Harmonica
- Already knows the basics and want to proceed further in Harmonica
- Intermediate & Advanced learners in Harmonica
- Parents & Teachers to teach Harmonica to the next generation
- Harmonica Lovers
- Music Lovers

2.2 What makes this book different and unique from others

Well there are plenty of books in Harmonica available in Amazon. So then, why need to write another book? First of all, it's the blessings from Guruji Sri D Madhusudan for preparing me as a music Teacher. With Guru's wish, this book has the research work on Harmonica. The salient features of this book are truly unique and slowly the reader will reach their goal with proper techniques.

- **Notations available in 3 Ways – Sheet Music, Harmonica Tabs and Indian Notes together**

You will not get another book following multiple notations in the market, because it needs tremendous effort & perfections. Our objective is to keep the notation flexible to the learner, such that you can follow the notation of your own choice. Few basic conventions are needed to understand from staff notes for the beating patterns, and this book covers them as well.

- **Beginners, Intermediate & Advanced Lessons together in this single book**

Starting from Prelims, then Beginners, Intermediate & Advanced, over 40 lessons are in this single book. The lessons, rather songs and tunes are organized in such a way that the learner can gradually discover new pointers. Each lesson shows the key learning benefits from that tune or song. The Notation Lyrics are also given for reader's benefit to memorize better. Some of the songs have the touch of interlude music and that pattern of playing will attract any learner. You will learn the Chromatic Harmonica in a systematic way.

> **Various Genre and Rhythmic patterns: Music from all over the world**

The book cover will show you the glimpse of the Genres used in the book. For instance, Children Music, Folk Music, Country, Bollywood Songs, Indian Folk, Soft Rock, Jazz, Christmas Songs, Waltz, Music for Marching, Dorian Music, Phrygian mode etc will enrich the learns skill with different patterns on notes & rhythms.

> **Further Learning at the end of every level**

Whenever any section ends (Either of Beginner, Intermediate or Advanced), further learning's are illustrated with more songs initial or first line's tune or notes. That will help the learner to choose more songs and initiate playing from their own. Idea of 15 more songs have been given which can be selected and played on Harmonica. The first lines of the songs were given to pick up. That will help the learner to find the song by own.

2.3   Time to achieve the milestones

> **Preliminary Lessons including Notation Conventions ~ 1 month**
> **Beginners Lessons ~ 2 months**
> **Intermediate Lessons ~ 2 – 3 months**
> **Advanced Lessons ~ 3 – 4 months**

Overall, you can finish all lessons within 8 months to 1 year. Only effort needed is daily minimum of 30 minutes of practice. After every lesson, you can compare your learning with the key learning points mentioned in the book. Every lesson has been gradually set to achieve some new goals. Completion of all lessons will help you to play and perform independently.

You can tag your Audio / Video recording with hash tag "#MouthOrganForEveryoneBook" in social media and so that we can see you playing.

2.4   About the Notations

All of the notations are arranged here considering the best fit for a **C Scaled Chromatic Harmonica**. The notations are ordered in a gradual learning curriculum which will be fast and easy to pick up by a Harmonica player. These notations may not be 100 % exact with the original notation as we have to reduce the complexity for Harmonica. Some of them have more Harmonica flavour with chord style playing. Notations contain the lyrics for helping the learner. It was really a hard work to construct the notations for overall 40 lessons including songs and tunes and that too in 3 flavours – **Staff Notes, Harmonica Tabs and Indian Notes**. Hope you will enjoy the outcome. Happy practicing 😊

3.0   Introduction to Harmonica

The name of the instrument, **Harmonica**, tells us that it's to create Harmony. It's also called as **Mouth Organ** as the source of sound comes from mouth. Harmonica is the type **Free Reeds** in the instrumental classification. The inflow or outflow of air in the instrument causes reeds to vibrate and that causes the sound.

It's the one of the most compact instrument with highest quality. A standard Harmonica contains 2, 3 or max 4 octaves within very short length. For example, a 2.5 Octave (10 Hole) harmonica length can be smaller than the Pen in which I am writing.

3.1   Why this can be your choice of instrument

First of all it's too easy to start the Harmonica. Anyone can make sound of it. Whenever you give a little effort, you can produce melody & rhythm. Slowly you can learn most of the basics by yourselves. Highlighting some of the interesting part of Harmonica which other instruments are lacking –

- **Melodious sound** → Even if you don't know how to play, you will produce melodious sound in Harmonica.
- **Quick to Pickup** → Once you grab the 7 notes, you can play the songs and rhythms quickly.
- **Easy to carry** → Nothing to mention about it as compared to other instruments, you can carry it easily in your pocket or backpack. So you can play while you are travelling, or you are at your school or even at your playground, anywhere.
- **Controlling the volume** → Once gaining blowing quality, you will love the bold sound of the single note or a group of notes. Similarly you will get to know the variation by controlling the air volume with your hand and blowing or drawing force on each note. Very few instruments have this feature (for example: touch effect on Digital Piano).
- **Lower Investment** → You can start with an average quality Harmonica with a lower investment. Once you discover your potential, then you can easily go for a better one.

3.2   How many sounds in a position

Because of the compactness, the Diatonic Harmonica has 2 sounds in every position – one with blowing (exhale) & another one with drawing (inhale) the air. When the key or sliding bar is pressed, the **Chromatic Harmonica** has 2 more sounds and **so it contains a total of 4 sounds** in each position or every hole.

These are all with the assumption that, artist is playing through single hole from mouth (lips). If multiple holes are played, for instance in case of playing accompanying with Chords, then multiple sounds will come out.

So you can feel that Harmonica needs quite perfection from other instruments. But that is actually not at all a concern to the Harmonica players. Because the hands & lips position, the blowing power of all notes will be automatically in the reflex & memorized in the players mind. Within 6 months of regular practice, a harmonica player can gain the control of playing songs or tunes or notations without thinking on – whether to blow now, whether to draw now, whether to press the sliding bar button etc. It's all attained in natural human reflex.

3.3   Full of Harmony

From the term Harmonica, it's always full of Harmony. It can't generate a noisy sound if anyone only blows along the length of Harmonica. Even it gives Harmony if someone only draws air along the length of it. The instrument is designed in such a nice manner.

On this context, there is a nice story I remember. When I travel in airlines, I always carry the Harmonica in the Cabin Luggage. But, any security person generally always catches the bag. They ask to open and show all items. Finally when we reach till Harmonica, I need to open the box and play some tune or song.

Once, I was in a hurry, and upon catching the bag, I opened the Harmonica and quickly played by blowing from left to right side. Then the security person told me – "Hello Master that can be played by anyone. Play some known tune." After that, I played the famous Bollywood song - "**Hai Aapna Dil**" and then he released the bag.

So, Harmonica can be played by anyone. It will always produce positive note or combination of notes even if you don't know how to play. With such an interesting design of the instrument, it's by default tuned with the Harmonic Chords of the desired scale if you only blow or only draw. We love the instrument for this Harmony.

3.4   Types of Harmonica & Purposes

There are 3 different types of Harmonica which are used in general.

3.4.1   Diatonic Harmonica:

Diatonic Harmonica is set for playing one Key (scale) at one time. It's popular for note bending techniques which are common on western style of music. For Europe & North American countries, Diatonic Harmonica is also termed as Blues Harmonica.

Figure 2: Diatonic Harmonica – Blues master from Suzuki on the Key Db / C#

Following are the supported Notes on a **10 Hole Diatonic Harmonica**.

For detailed reference on octaves on the Key (scale) of C ➔

- **Middle octave contains all Major Note**
- **Lower Octave does not contain F & A**

➤ Higher Octave does not contain B

blow	C	E	G	C	E	G	C	E	G	C
holes	1	2	3	4	5	6	7	8	9	10
draw	D	G	B	D	F	A	B	D	F	A

<== Lower Octave ==> <== Middle Octave ==> <== Higher Octave ==>

Table 1: Diatonic Harmonica from Suzuki - Blowing Positions with Notes on the Key of C

Purpose & Utility: Diatonic Harmonica is primarily used for note bending; accompany music, playing rhythm, chords & harmony. You can easily accompany with the chords here as you can try C, G, G7, Dm etc chords with playing multiple notes from your mouth coverage. For example –

- ➤ C Chord ➔ C E G C can be played together by blowing 1234 holes
- ➤ G Chord ➔ D G B D can be played together by drawing 1234 holes
- ➤ G7 Chord ➔ G B D F can be played together by drawing 2345 holes
- ➤ Dm Chord ➔ D F A can be played together by drawing 456 holes
- ➤ F Chord ➔ F A can be played together by drawing 5 6 holes. That will reach nearer to F Chord. You can also play in 2 quick beats like one by blowing on C and then the second by drawing on F & A to give the F chord based rhythm.

Limitations:

You can't play Minor or Sharp notes easily in Diatonic Harmonica for example – C#, D#, F#, G# & A#. With the note bending technique, you can try playing closure to some of them using note bending.

All of the major notes, in lower and higher octave, may not be present. Check the above Table for details.

3.4.2 Chromatic Harmonica

Chromatic Harmonica is named for its coverage of Chromatic Notes that is all 12 notes in an octave. Chromatic Harmonica with a changer key only contains 12 notes. Without the changer key, a Chromatic Harmonica contains all 7 Major notes within the Octave. As earlier specified a Harmonica contains 2 or 3 or max 4 Octaves.

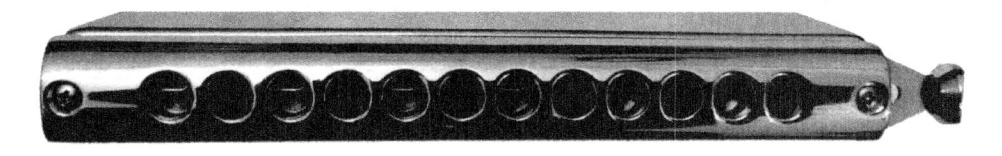

Figure 3: The Chromatic Harmonica

Notes are given below for a standard **Chromatic Harmonica of 10 Holes** of C scale and also containing the Changer Key –

				<== Middle Octave ==>						
blow	C#	F	G#	C#	F	G#	C#	F	G#	Key In
blow	C	E	G	C	E	G	C	E	G	Key out
holes	1	2	3	4	5	6	7	8	9	10
draw	D	F	A	B	D	F	A	B	D	F	Key out
draw	D#	F#	A#	C	D#	F#	A#	C	D#	F#	Key in

<== Lower Octave ==>   <= Higher Octave =>

Table 2: Chromatic Harmonica - Blowing Positions with Notes on the Key of C

To compare the size of the Harmonica with the Octaves, following bullets will help

- **10 Hole Chromatic Harmonica → 2.5 Octaves as depicted in the diagram**
- **12 Hole Chromatic Harmonica → 3 Octaves**
- **16 Hole Chromatic Harmonica → 4 Octaves**

For a Beginner, 10 Hole Chromatic Harmonica will be good enough to start with.

Purpose & Utility:

- **Chromatic Harmonica can be played for Lead Music, Cover songs, Bollywood songs, Western Pop, Rock, Jazz Music, Folk, Country, Western Classical and even Indian Classical to some extent.**
- **It can be also played for simulating the Chord or accompanying with the Rhythm.**
- **Due to all 12 sounds, it can play anything you want. But, Mouth Organs are not a good choice on those songs which has too many Minor notes.**

Limitations:

- **The Diatonic has more Chord combinations than Chromatic based on the scale. That is explained in the Diatonic one with illustrations.**
- **If you are trying for Note Bending techniques, some Diatonic versions may better than Chromatic as it contains both the reeds on same note and that turns out better bending sounds. This limitation can be overcome with better quality Chromatic Harmonica like the one from Hohner or Suzuki.**

3.4.3 Tremolo Harmonica

Tremolo Harmonica are the diatonic type Harmonica originated at East Asian Countries. Tremolo Harmonica generally has 2 reeds per note. The two reeds are tuned slightly off a reference pitch with one being slightly sharp and the other being slightly flat. That produces the unique wavering or warbling sound created by the two reeds. It can give us the beautiful melody & rhythm on the East Asian music & tunes. In our childhood days, 30 years back, this is the one which was available by default in eastern Indian also. We used to play the dark green coloured Tremolo Harmonica.

Figure 4: Tremolo Harmonica from Easttop

Blow	G^3		C^4		E^4		G^4		C^5		E^5		G^5		C^6		E^6		G^6		C^7		E^7	
holes	1	2	3	4	5	6	7	8	9	10	11	12	13	14	15	16	17	18	19	20	21	22	23	24
Draw		D^4		F^4		A^4		B^4		D^5		F^5		A^5		B^5		D^6		F^6		A^6		B^6

Table 3: Tremolo Harmonica - East Asian Tuning - Blowing Positions with Notes on the Key of C

Blow	C		E		G		C		E		G		C		E		G		C	
Hohner's Lebel	1		2		3		4		5		6		7		8		9		10	
Standard Label	1	2	3	4	5	6	7	8	9	10	11	12	13	14	15	16	17	18	19	20
Draw		D		G		B		D		F		A		B		D		F		A

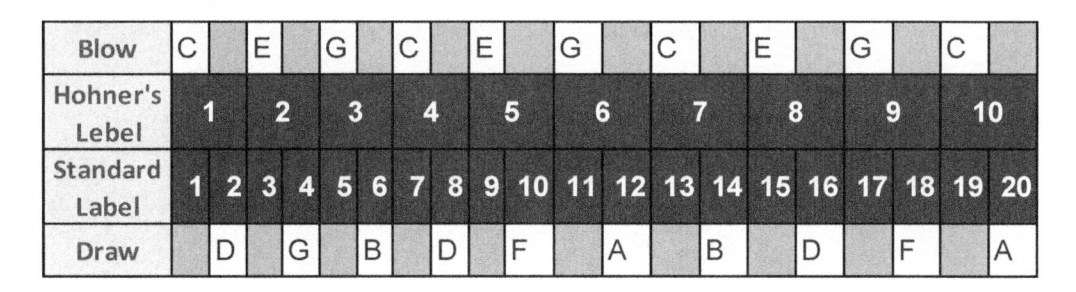

Table 4: Tremolo Harmonica – Asian Tuning – Blowing Positions with Notes on the Key of C

Purpose & Use:

Tremolo Harmonica's are majorly used for Folk Music in East Asian countries like China, Japan, Taiwan, Korea etc. We can find the reference of Tremolo Harmonica in European countries also in the folk music, traditional folk, classical music etc. The beating can be easily achieved in Tremolo Harmonica.

Limitations:

- **The primary drawback is no scale changing option. So most of the Indian music or western music with minor notes may not be easy to play in Tremolo Harmonica.**

Out of these 3 types of harmonicas, we will primarily focus on **Chromatic Harmonica** in our book with its capability to play any music.

3.5 Style of Playing, Special Effects

3.5.1 Holding Technique –

Cover your left hand completely from the top of instrument and so your right hand will be free. It can be used to create special effect of Vibrato or Vibration. Also use your right thumb to apply Key Change for the Minor notes in Chromatic Harmonica.

Figure 5: Holding Technique using Right Hand Thumb for Key changing

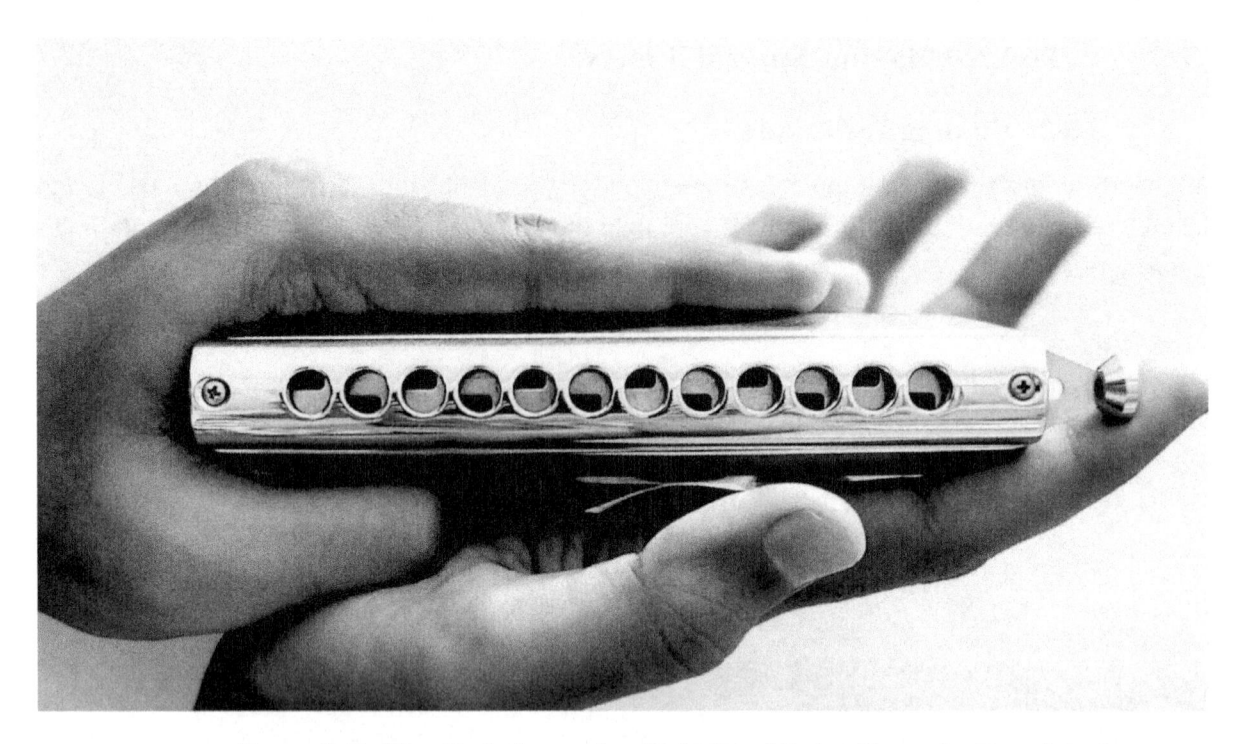

Figure 6: Holding Technique using Right Hand Index Finger for Key changing

You can hold with either of these techniques with your flexibility. Make sure the right hand is flexible to cover the back of Harmonica for Vibration effect.

3.5.2 Whistle Style:

This is the most common style to blow like Whistle. With this whistle style, your lips will be touching the Harmonica and with the round shaped hole in between your lips, you have to draw or blow air. We recommend playing with this technique most of the time for the tropical or humid countries.

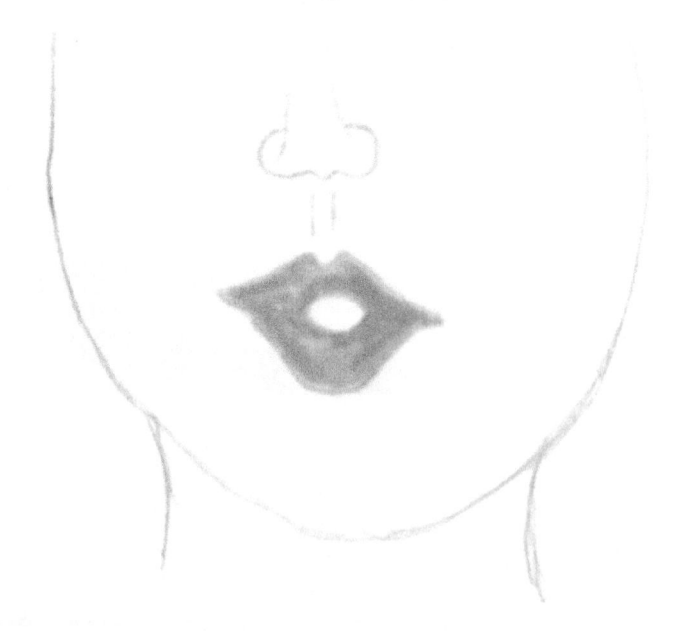

Figure 7: The whistle style

3.5.3 Tongue Assist Style:

This is the technique to user your tongue to cover the Holes and keep the desired one open.

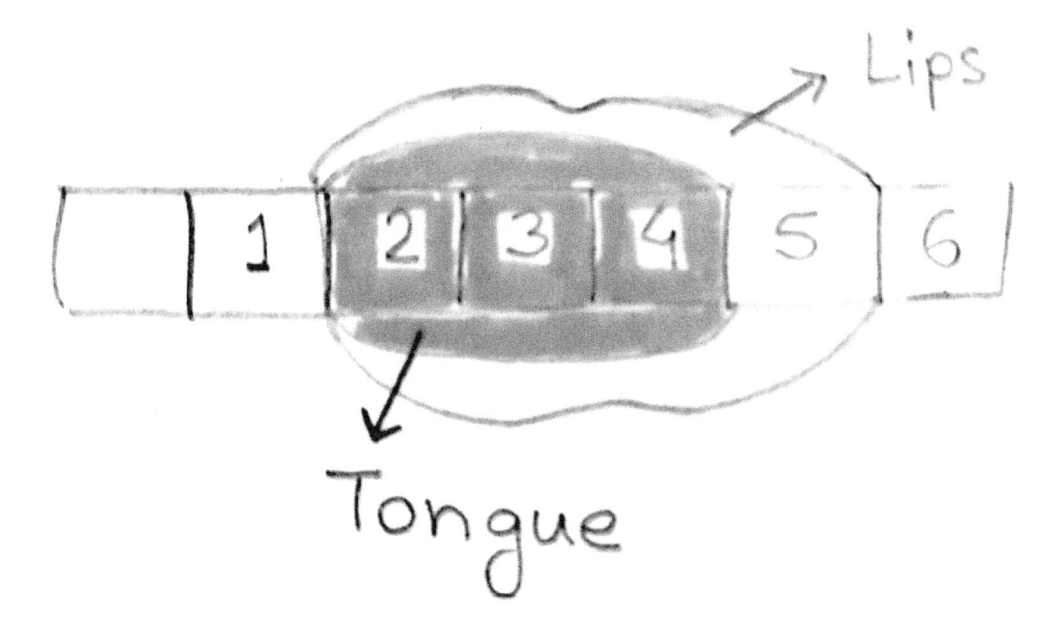

Figure 8: The tongue assist style

- **Lips to cover around 4 Holes**
- **Tongue can block 3 Holes and allow the blowing or drawing wind to flow the remaining one Hole. Example, here in the above diagram, the hole number 5 is used to play as hole numbers 2, 3 and 4 are blocked by tongue.**
- **It can be either left or right of tongue as given in the texture.**

This technique can add water / saliva particles inside Harmonica. So it's not recommended at humid areas to avoid damages of your Harmonica.

3.5.4 Special Effects: Vibrato

Vibrato or vibration effect can be achieved with your right hand finger movements. As given in the Figure 2, use your right hand to open & close your palm or fingers to allow or block air. Vibrato can be used in place of sustaining music or chords.

3.5.5 Special Effects: Bending

Note bending or pitch bending is the technique of changing the pitch or frequency of the note. You can easily achieve in harmonica controlling the following –

- **Slight position change of the Harmonica from your lips**
- **Air pressure change or kind of chocking while blowing or drawing**

Example: The original note in the drawing of 1st Hole position is D. Using the node Bending, you can achieve a raise in frequency from D to D#.

3.6 Which model to buy (for Beginner)

The companies like **Jewels, Tower** have Chromatic Harmonicas from Rs 500 – 1k (Around 10 USD). Those can be initially fine, but those are not professional harmonica. After 3 to 6 month, you should change to a better one.

- Tower Mouth Organ Harmonica 24 Holes Key-C With Scale Change Option, Silver - https://www.amazon.in/dp/B00QGDYE20
- JUAREZ 24 Holes JRH24CHBL Harmonica Brass Reed Plate Aluminium Cover Chromatic Tower Mouth Organ With case Blue https://www.amazon.in/dp/B08JW1N3KC/

Next better quality ones are from brands **Conjurer, Easttop, Swan** etc. Starting range of them are from 2k to 5k INR (starts from 30 USD). Example:

- **Conjurer Chromatic 12 Hole** - https://www.amazon.in/dp/B09YPZ2CQ2
- **Easttop Chromatic Harmonica 10 hole** - https://www.amazon.in/Easttop-T10-40-Mouth-Organ-Harmonica/
- **Swan Chromatic Harmonica 12 hole** - https://www.amazon.in/Swan-Hole-Chromatic-Harmonica-SW1248/dp/B00P7ESYU2

Best Quality Harmonicas are from **Hohner** and **Suzuki**. Those have price range starting from 12k INR (starts from 100 USD). These are the professional ones. The breath to sound efficiency is also much better when you play these professional one. I mean the less breath force is needed and better quality sound will produce with minimum effort. Note bending techniques are also easily established.

Initial versions from these companies are

- **Hohner Chromatic Harmonica** - https://www.amazon.in/dp/B00LE6JFGY
- **Suzuki Chromatic Harmonica** - https://www.amazon.in/dp/B00133A19S/

We always suggest taking the Chromatic Harmonica from middle range like **Conjurer, Easttop or Swan** to start with. 10 holes Harmonica should be fine and support 80 - 90% of the professional need. Those are also very good quality and you can perform on stage with those. Gradually after 3-4 years, you can shift to **Hohner** or **Suzuki**.

By default the Harmonica scale will be C. That will also cover C# scale if you use the scale changer. You should start with your C Harmonica. If you are only building your career as Harmonica player, then you can purchase the following major scales gradually 5 – 10 years of your journey.

- D (covers D# / Eb)
- E (covers F)
- G (covers G#)
- A (covers A# / Bb)

For reference, we are just an observer for the external links of products. The links of these products were available on or before Dec 2022 in Indian Amazon and they may be valid till their business policy. At US, Europe, UK, Canada or worldwide, same products may be available with different Amazon link or from different musical stores. So, please search with the name and type of the product which you want to buy and collect the latest model.

3.7　　Small tips to take care of your harmonica

- **Brush your teeth before playing. Use fine cotton to clean the blowing holes externally.**
- **If any hole is stuck with moisture, try to use an ear bud to clean the moisture externally.**
- **Keep a small pouch of Silica Gel (available at Medicine shops) in the Harmonica box to capture moisture. Kids should take parental guidance before using Silica Gel pouch.**
- **Keep your Harmonica at Dry place and sometimes under morning sunlight.**

4.0 Notations Conventions

Notation conventions are really needed for you to able to read the Notes and play. The advantage of this book is, it will be providing you 3 types of notation

- **Staff Notes / Sheet Music**
- **Harmonica Tablature / Tabs**
- **Indian Notes**

4.1 About the Middle C and Octaves:

Harmonica has generally 2.5 Octaves (10 Hole) to 3 Octaves (12 Hole). Well there are lot of definitions of Harmonica Tabs as within Harmonica also there are plenty of tunings across the world. We will follow the Standard Chromatic Harmonica Tablature conventions.

To get the best view of the Harmonica Tabs in align with the staff notes, we have arrived on the below convention. Most of the song notes starts from Lower Octave G (Pa), then Middle Octave and to the maximum, it goes till Higher Octave G (Pa). So we have chosen the Middle Octave from Harmonica tabs (+4) (Indian Note S) in the staff notes Middle C where it's most coverage on the staff lines.

By Octave sound wise, it can vary + / – 1 octave for some cases. Ex: Some of the Chromatic Harmonica has the middle octave from C6 / Ŝ position (One octave shift from the table) whereas most of the Chromatic Harmonica has the **middle octave from C5 / S position** (same as the table). But if we follow the higher octave one, readability of the Staff notes may not be good as it will be mostly on the upper side. Hence the below one is the most convention for Harmonica to follow the notes.

Both 10 or 12 Hole Chromatic Harmonica will contain middle octave C / S (Sa note) in both Holes: **4th and 5th position**. Similarly a 12 Hole Chromatic Harmonica, will contain higher octave C / S (Sa note) in both **8th and 9th Hole position**. But in **10 Hole** Chromatic Harmonica, you will have only one Hole for higher octave C / S (Sa note), and that is **8th** Hole. Refer **Table 2 (Page 12) for 10 Hole Harmonica**. Refer the next page, "**Note symbols 1**", for **12 Hole Harmonica**.

From the below table, we can understand the relation between all conventions and their position in 12 Hole Chromatic Harmonica.

Western Note	Piano Octave Number	Harmonica Symbol	Blow / Draw Air	Is Major	Indian Notation Symbol	Indian Swar Details	Octave Position
C	4	+1	Blow	Y	S̱	Sa	Lower
C# / Db	4	+1s	Blow	N	ṟ	Komal re	Lower
D	4	-1	Draw	Y	Ṟ	Re	Lower
D# / Eb	4	-1s	Draw	N	g̱	Komal ga	Lower
E	4	+2	Blow	Y	G̱	Ga	Lower
F	4	-2	Draw	Y	m̱	ma	Lower
F# / Gb	4	-2s	Draw	N	M̱	Tibra Ma	Lower
G	4	+3	Blow	Y	P̱	Pa	Lower
G# / Ab	4	+3s	Blow	N	ḏ	Komal dha	Lower
A	4	-3	Draw	Y	Ḏ	Dha	Lower
A# / Bb	4	-3s	Draw	N	ṉ	Komal ni	Lower
B	4	-4	Draw	Y	Ṉ	Ni	Lower
C	4	+4	Blow	Y	S	Sa	Lower
C	5	+5	Blow	Y	S	Sa	Middle
C# / Db	5	+4s or +5s	Blow	N	r	Komal re	Middle
D	5	-5	Draw	Y	R	Re	Middle
D# / Eb	5	-5s	Draw	N	g	Komal ga	Middle
E	5	+6	Blow	Y	G	Ga	Middle
F	5	-6	Draw	Y	m	ma	Middle
F# / Gb	5	-6s	Draw	N	M	Tibra Ma	Middle
G	5	+7	Blow	Y	P	Pa	Middle
G# / Ab	5	+7s	Blow	N	d	Komal dha	Middle
A	5	-7	Draw	Y	D	Dha	Middle
A# / Bb	5	-7s	Draw	N	n	Komal ni	Middle
B	5	-8	Draw	Y	N	Ni	Middle
C	6	+8	Blow	Y	Ŝ	Sa	Middle
C	6	+9	Blow	Y	Ŝ	Sa	Higher
C# / Db	6	+8s or +9s	Blow	N	ř	Komal re	Higher
D	6	-9	Draw	Y	R̂	Re	Higher
D# / Eb	6	-9s	Draw	N	ḡ	Komal ga	Higher
E	6	+10	Blow	Y	Ḡ	Ga	Higher
F	6	-10	Draw	Y	ḿ	ma	Higher
F# / Gb	6	-10s	Draw	N	Ḿ	Tibra Ma	Higher
G	6	+11	Blow	Y	Ṗ	Pa	Higher
G# / Ab	6	+11s	Blow	N	ḋ	Komal dha	Higher
A	6	-11	Draw	Y	Ḋ	Dha	Higher
A# / Bb	6	-11s	Draw	N	ṅ	Komal ni	Higher
B	6	-12	Draw	Y	Ṅ	Ni	Higher
C	7	+12	Blow	Y	Š	Sa	>>

Note Symbols 1: Octaves vs. all Notations (w.r.t. 12 Hole Chromatic Harmonica)

From the notation diagram, we can understand that,

- When we **inhale or draw air** from any hole, it's denoted with **minus "-" symbol**. Ex: "-5" means D or R (Re) in Indian Symbol.
- When we **exhale or blow** air, it's denoted as **"+" symbol**. Ex: "+4" means C or S (Sa) in Indian Symbol.
- Minor Notes contain the **slider symbol "s"** after the Hole number. Ex: "-5s" is the minor g and corresponding Sheet music location is given.
- Major Notes do not contain the symbol "s" after the Hole number. Couple of Major notes you can play using slider too. **It will be fun to discover that yourself**. Yes, you are right; it's the **m** (ma) and **S** (Sa). Please try and find the positions yourself. If you have any difficulties finding, you can send me a WhatsApp message too. Please refer to the last section – **Contact Page**.
- Octave numbers are just a reference point with Piano. It's for matching the Piano sound. In case you are a piano player too, you can compare the sound of your **Harmonica's middle octave** with **middle C in Piano** and send me a comment.

Once you are comfortable with middle Octave, from 4th – 8th Hole in Harmonica, it will be very easy for you to play lower / higher octave. You have to always follow your Harmonica's middle octave. Notations are just a path to help you to know the position of the notes.

There is nothing to worry, even if you do not know to read the Staff Notes. We will have 3 notations together in every notation diagram. So you will get to know the Harmonica Tab (Hole position with +/- symbol and slide key) and Indian Notes beneath every Staff Notes.

Notation Convention
Staff Notes vs Harmonica Tabs vs Indian Notes

by Riddhi Sanyal

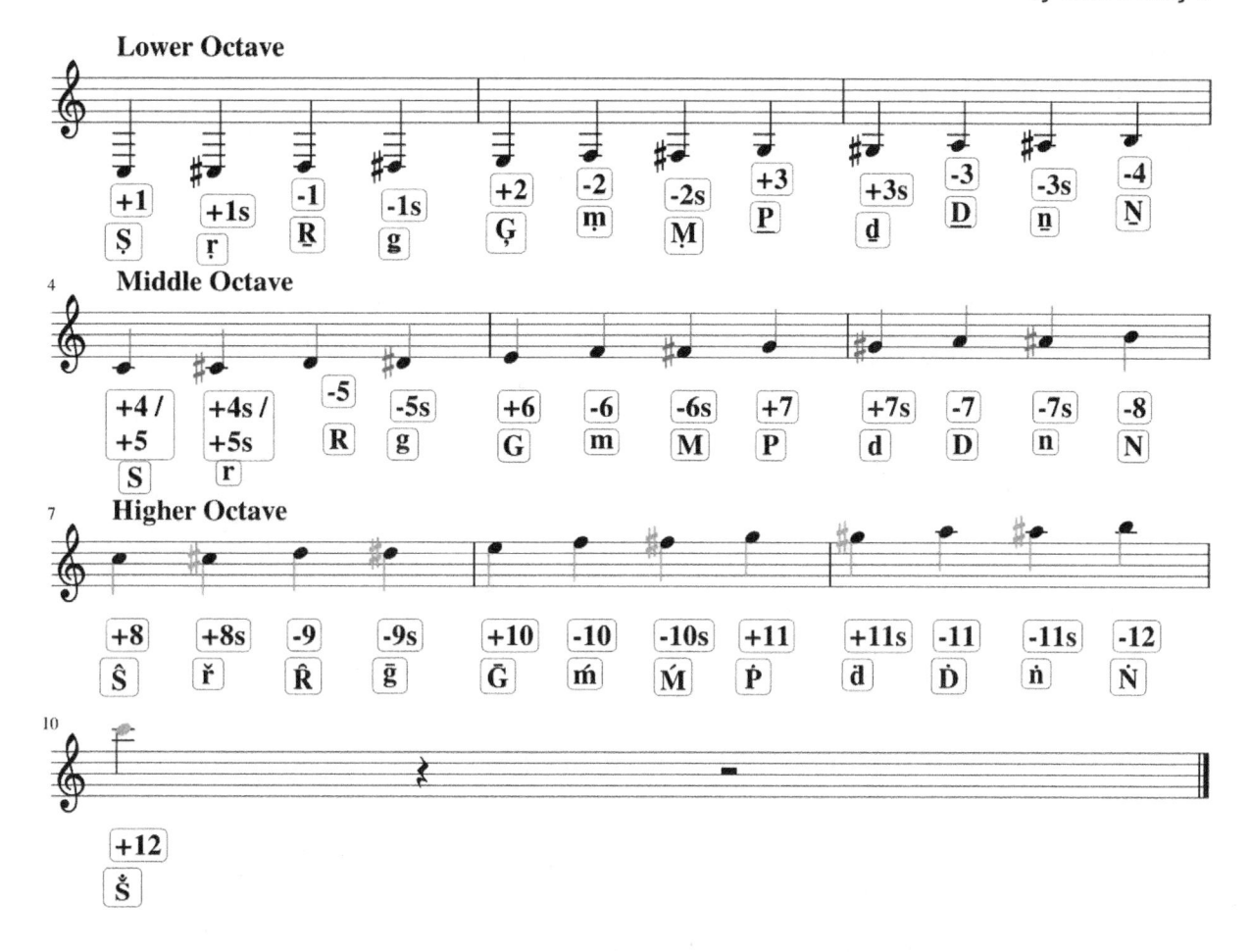

Note Symbols 2: Notation Conventions – All Possible Notes in 12 Hole Harmonica

– Staff Note vs. Harmonica Tabs vs. Indian Notes

4.2 The Most Played Major Notes

You may feel that, the above theoretical diagram is really complicated. Well the above diagram contains all possibilities of a Chromatic Harmonica with major (Slider Key off) and minor (Slider Key On). But practically, on a particular song, it's rare to have a tune or song where we have used all 12 notes within an octave. Even in the major notes, you may consider starting from lower Octave G / Pa Note (Symbol = ▯) and play upwards, complete the middle octave and then play till G / Pa (Symbol = Ṗ) Note of the Higher Octave. For simplicity, only major notes are listed in the following diagram. The notes given in the picture will be mostly played during our journey. You can say, more than 90% of the times, we will only play those major notes. Only 10% or lesser, we will focus on the minor notes.

Notation Convention - Major Notes Only
Staff Notes vs Harmonica Tabs vs Indian Notes
by Riddhi Sanyal

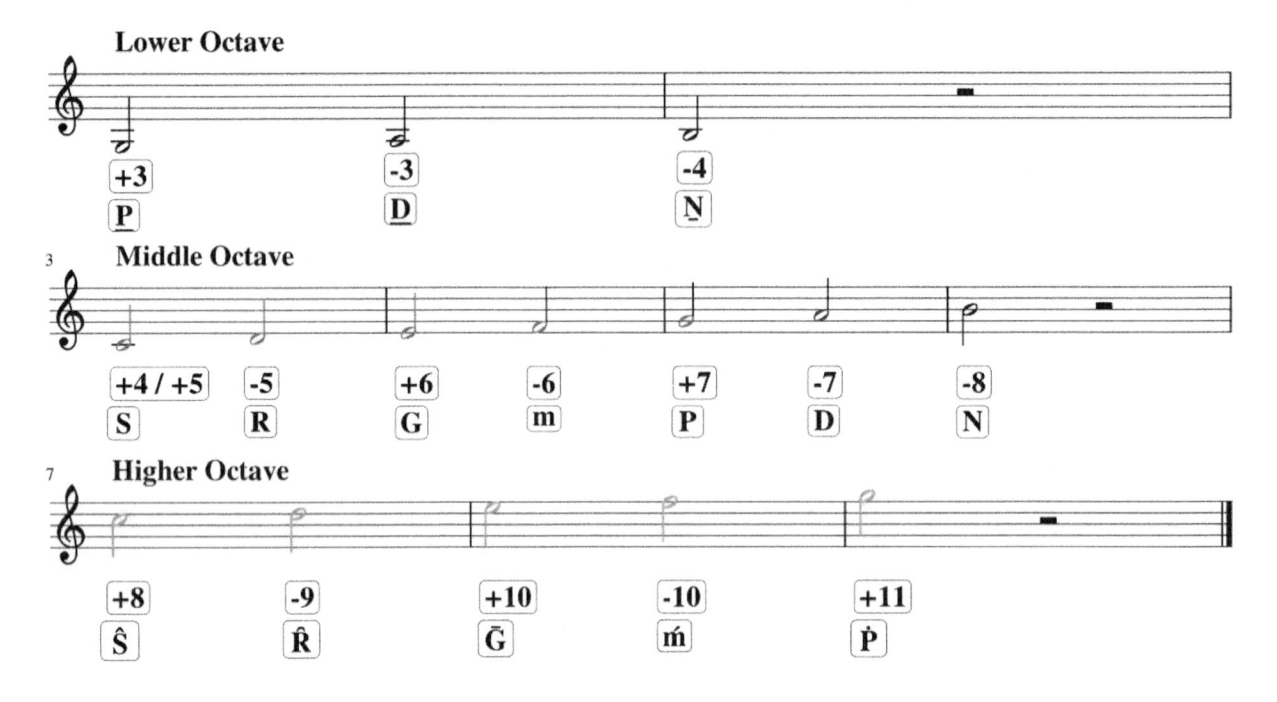

Lower Octave

+3 P
-3 D
-4 N

Middle Octave

+4 / +5 S
-5 R
+6 G
-6 m
+7 P
-7 D
-8 N

Higher Octave

+8 Ŝ
-9 R̂
+10 Ḡ
-10 ḿ
+11 Ṗ

Note Symbols 3: Notation Conventions – Mostly Played Major Notes

– Staff Note vs. Harmonica Tabs vs. Indian Notes

4.3   Staff Note symbols to remember

This section is only for those, who are absolutely new to the staff notes.

4.3.1 Clef & Staff Lines:

During our journey, we will always provide the Harmonica Tabs & Indian Notes along with the sheet music note position. Still from the reader's interest, few basics are given here.

The Treble clef is only required to know to play Harmonica. That is the musical notes part or right hand part of Piano. The 5 staff lines on a treble clef are formed in the notes of EGBDF. Gurudeb explains that to remember with the famous phrase "**Every Good Boy Does Fine**". Depicting the same in the picture:

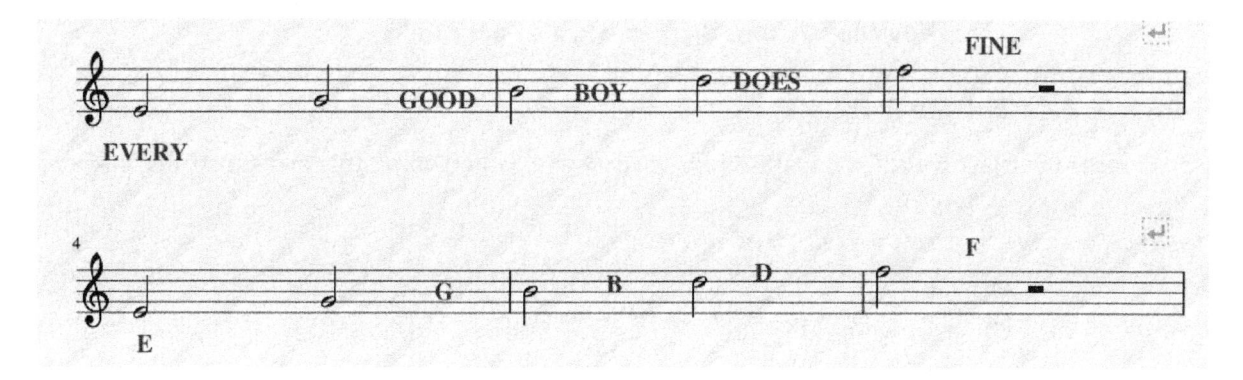

Note Symbols 4: Every Good Boy Does Fine – Learning Treble Clef

4.3.2 The Key Signature:

For Harmonica in C Scale, we will always follow the default Key Signature of C Major (A Minor) with 5 simple lines. You can ignore that for this book as there is no change in Key Signature. This is given to alert you when you read other staff notes.

Note Symbols 5: Key Signature

4.3.3 Time Signature:

The Time Signature is the pattern of Beats or Taal in Indian system. We have used 4/4 or Keherwa taal and 3/4 or Dadra Taal for most of the notation compositions. Same is given in the below pictures.

The 4/4 Beats or **Keherwa Taal**

Note Symbols 6: Time Signature 4/4 – Keherwa Taal

The 3/4 Beats or **Dadra Taal**

Note Symbols 7: Time Signature 3/4 – Dadra Taal

4.3.4 The Measure

The section or Phrase of a song, which is separated by vertical line, is known as the Measure. The following picture shows the measures 5th and 6th.

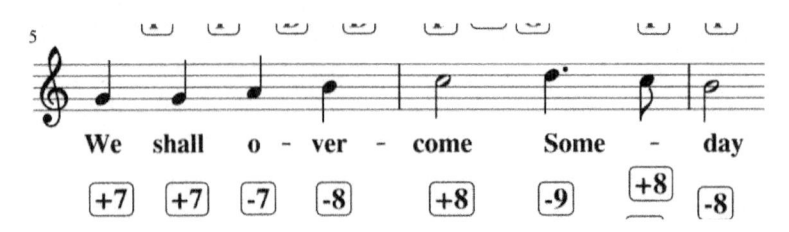

Note Symbols 8: Measures

4.3.5 The Note Symbols & Gaps

We need to closely observe this note symbols starting from Whole Note, then Half Note, Quarter Note, Eighth Note, Sixteenth Note. Similarly every note has a corresponding symbol for Gap / Rests. Following figure contains all of them together –

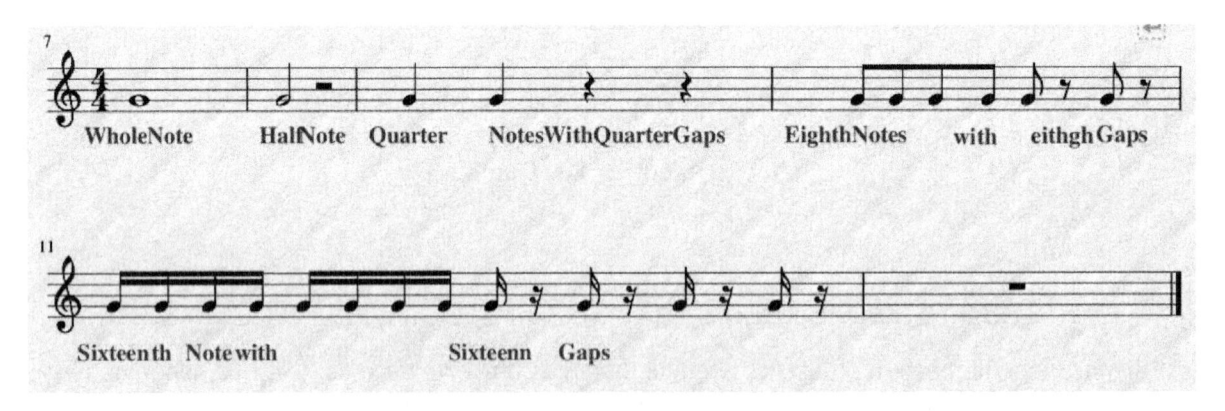

Note Symbols 9: Note Symbols & Gaps

To further illustrate, in a in 4/4 Time Signature –

- ➢ Whole Note is 4 beat in length. It's of oval shape.
- ➢ Half Note is 2/4 beat long.
- ➢ Quarter Note is 1/4 beat long and the time length is same with Quarter Gap.
- ➢ Eighth Note is 1/8 beat in length and time length is same with Eighth Gaps. When sequentially played, there will be a line joining the eighth Notes.
- ➢ Sixteenth Note is 1/16 beat in length and time length is same with Sixteenth Gap. When sequentially played, there will be 2 lines joining the Sixteenth Notes.

4.3.6 The Tempo:

The speed or Tempo is generally given for further illustration. Generally we have used the tempo from the Composers Guidance or from the actual speed of the song or tune. Initially you may practice in lower tempo and gradually play in the recommended or given tempo.

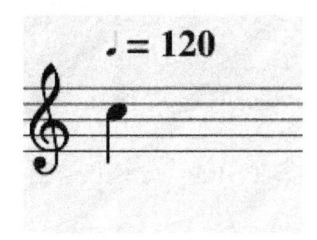

Note Symbols 10: The Tempo

Generally quarter note = 120 means, its 120 Beats per Minute. You can easily play with Tempo from any standard Metronome App.

4.3.7 The Dotted Note or Augmentation Dot

Every Dot will increase the duration of that note by 1.5 times. Single Dot is very common when you want to give stress or sustain more on a part of lyrics. This can be easily understood from the simple song "Row Row Row Your Boat".

Note Symbols 11: Dotted Notes

See the phrase "Row your" or "Gent - ly" or "down the". Each of these word or phrase has more sustain on the first word or phrase. So, those are added with Dots to increase the time span of that word.

4.3.8 Repeats

When a section or verse replicates, it's represented as repeats in Sheet Music. Well repeats are the way of representing the notation in a compact way. Readers can easily find that repeated section and the length of the notation are reduced and hence effort of reader is reduced too.

Few of the ways of repeats are given below –

One Measure is repeated: Here in this below diagram, the measure 13 is repeated with a divide symbol.

Note Symbols 12: Measure is repeated

Any Verse is repeated: Here in this diagram the measures 15 to 19 are repeated with the surrounding Repeat Symbols as highlighted below.

Symbols 13: Verse is repeated

Repeat & Continue from another point:

This can be achieved in various codes. One of the examples with "D. S. al Coda" is given below.

We can see from the below diagram that, "D. S. al Coda" is present at the measure number 26. So, from this measure 26, we have to go back to Segno Symbol (measure 15). Play until "To Coda" which is at measure 22. Then continue from the Coda symbol at measure 27.

So that's how we can play to certain point and jump to another section. This is how the Verse 1 or *Bandish* (*Sthyai*) sections are given in the real song or tunes.

Note Symbols 14: Repeat and jump to another section

4.3.9 Further readings are listed as Reference:

We have learned most of the basics which are required to proceed with Harmonica. Again, due to alternative notations (Harmonica Tabs & Indian Notes), it will be always easy for anyone to follow the Notation. Only for time signature, time length of note, length of gaps, repeats, tempo, etc, you have to understand the sheet music. Interested learners can read the further learning links given here.

- Reading Sheet Music from https://www.wikihow.com/Read-Piano-Sheet-Music
- Notation Symbols from https://en.wikipedia.org/wiki/List_of_musical_symbols
- Dotted Note from https://en.wikipedia.org/wiki/Dotted_note
- Repeats can be referred from https://en.wikipedia.org/wiki/Repeat_sign
- Da Capo Repeats can be referred from https://en.wikipedia.org/wiki/Da_capo

5.0 Preliminary lessons for Harmonica

Learning Period for the Preliminary Lessons:

➢ This section will take approximately 15 – 20 days of your days of practice assuming you can pick up one lesson within 1 - 2 days.

➢ You should complete the further learning section of 2 more patterns by 5 days.

➢ At max, if you sincerely practice daily for at least 30 minutes of your time, you can complete the Preliminary section within 1 month.

5.1 Learn the Octaves and play the middle OCTAVE

By default the Harmonica scale will be C unless you specifically opt for a different one. Hence C scale will be followed in this book.

Start from the middle C (Sa) and play the middle octave (*highlighted*). We will only play the major notes to start with. When we will play the major notes, key change will never be pressed (Key out position). So you need to blow and draw gently for consecutive notes. There is only one exception. After drawing the A Major note (Indian note Dha), the B Major note (Indian note Ni) has to be drawn too. Please note that, the middle C (Sa) can be played while blowing at any of the holes 4 & 5.

To simplify the playing with blow & draw air, you can follow this table for 10 Hole Harmonica –

				<== Middle Octave ==>							
Blow	C	E	G	C	C	E	G	C	E	G	Key out
holes	1	2	3	4	5	6	7	8	9	10	
Draw	D	F	A	B	D	F	A	B	D	F	Key out
	<== Lower Octave ==>					<= Higher Octave =>					

Table 5: Play middle octave (western notes)

				<== Middle Octave ==>							
Blow	Ṣ	G̣	□	S	S	G	P	Ŝ	Ḡ	Ṗ	Key out
holes	1	2	3	4	5	6	7	8	9	10	
Draw	R̲	m	D̲	N̲	R	m	D	N	R̂	ṁ	Key out
	<== Lower Octave ==>					<= Higher Octave =>					

Table 6: Play middle octave (Indian notes)

When we play in simple Metronome App, setting 4/4 beats; we can map this into simple sheet music. Every note is represented as Quarter Notes here. The advantage of this book is that, you can always refer to Harmonica Tabs and Indian Notes in parallel with the sheet music.

So we will play the middle octave in both ascending and descending order. The tempo can be very low initially like 60 – 80 BPM.

Play Middle Octave in 4/4

- Harmonica Tabs
- Indian notes
- by Riddhi Sanyal

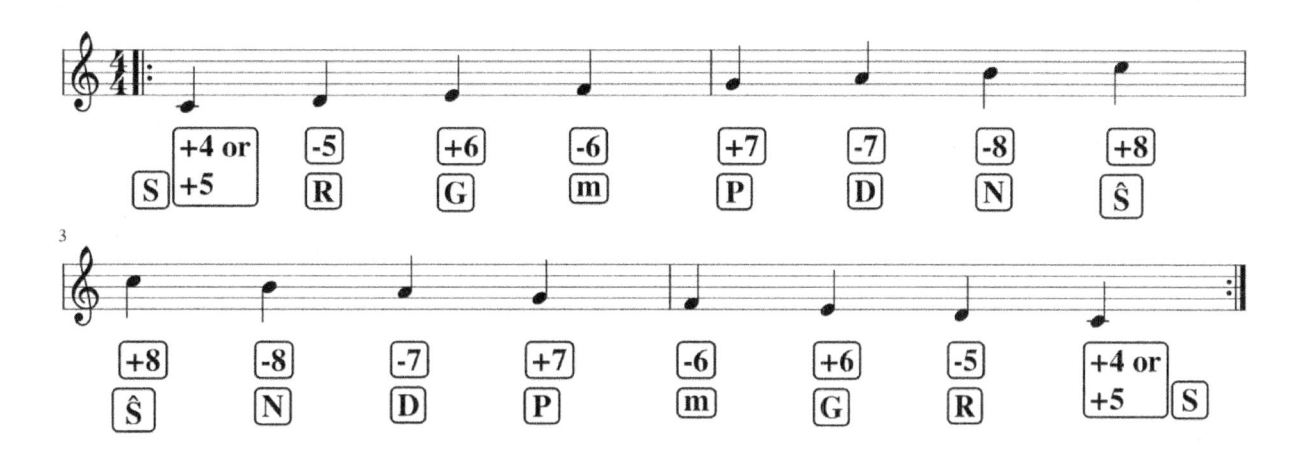

+4 or +5	-5	+6	-6	+7	-7	-8	+8
S	R	G	m	P	D	N	Ŝ

+8	-8	-7	+7	-6	+6	-5	+4 or +5
Ŝ	N	D	P	m	G	R	S

Lesson 1: Play Middle Octave

Once you are comfortable on the entire middle octave, you can add some notes from lower and higher octave. From the earlier illustration on most played notes in Section 3.2, we will now practice the same in ascending and descending order in the similar tempo with 4/4 beat Metronome. To form in 4/4 rhythm, we will play the C or S (Sa) note two times.

Practice this at least 30 – 40 times in one session. Then you can increase the tempo gradually.

Add Lower & Higher Octave Notes with Middle Octave in 4/4

- Harmonica Tabs
- Indian notes
- by Riddhi Sanyal

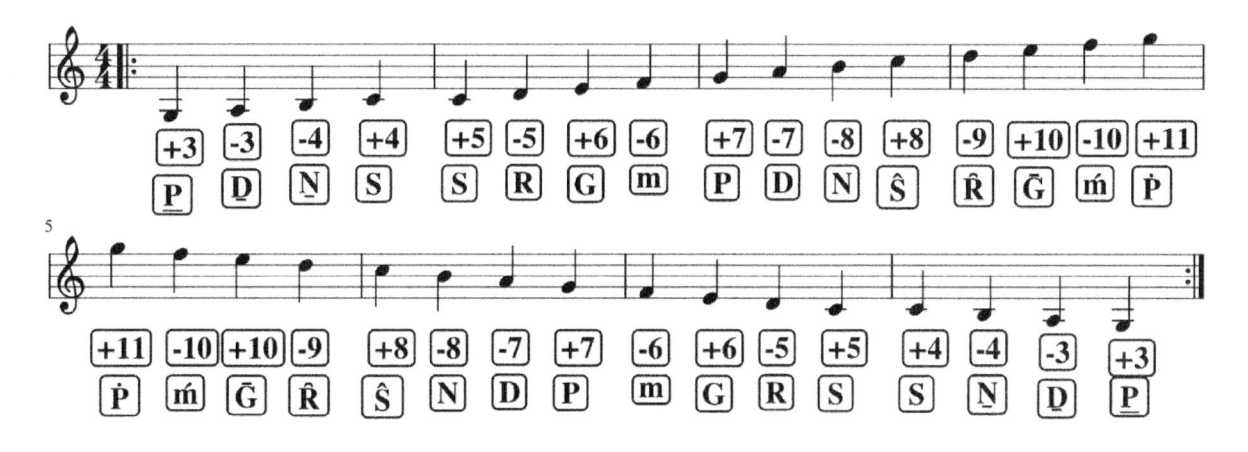

+3	-3	-4	+4	+5	-5	+6	-6	+7	-7	-8	+8	-9	+10	-10	+11
P̱	Ḏ	Ṉ	S	S	R	G	m	P	D	N	Ŝ	R̂	Ĝ	m̂	P̂

+11	-10	+10	-9	+8	-8	-7	+7	-6	+6	-5	+5	+4	-4	-3	+3
P̂	m̂	Ĝ	R̂	Ŝ	N	D	P	m	G	R	S	S	Ṉ	Ḏ	P̱

Lesson 2: Add Lower & Higher Octave Notes with Middle Octave & Play in 4/4

5.2   Play two same notes at a Time

Once you are comfortable on the middle octave, you can start playing 2 notes at a time. Please try to follow equal time signature for all notes. To explain, give same time interval (pause) between each note, so that you will gradually learn to play in rhythm. This exercise can be played with a simple 4/4 Beat with a simple Metronome App.

For the initial days, you can keep the tempo very low as 60 – 80 (Beats per Minute).

In staff notation, this practice is shown with couple of speed or tempo. The starting 16 measures are shown with **Half (1/2) Notes**. Next 8 measures, from 17 – 24, the same notes are changed into **Quarter (1/4) notes**. Therefore, the playing tempo should be double while playing the measures from 17 – 24. Hence, you should start with very show tempo like 60 – 80 BPM. Then you should be able to play both sections of the staff notation 1. The staff notation / sheet music will help the learners to be comfortable on the notation conventions of Half note & Quarter notes.

Playing 2 Notes at a time

- Harmonica Notes
- by Riddhi Sanyal

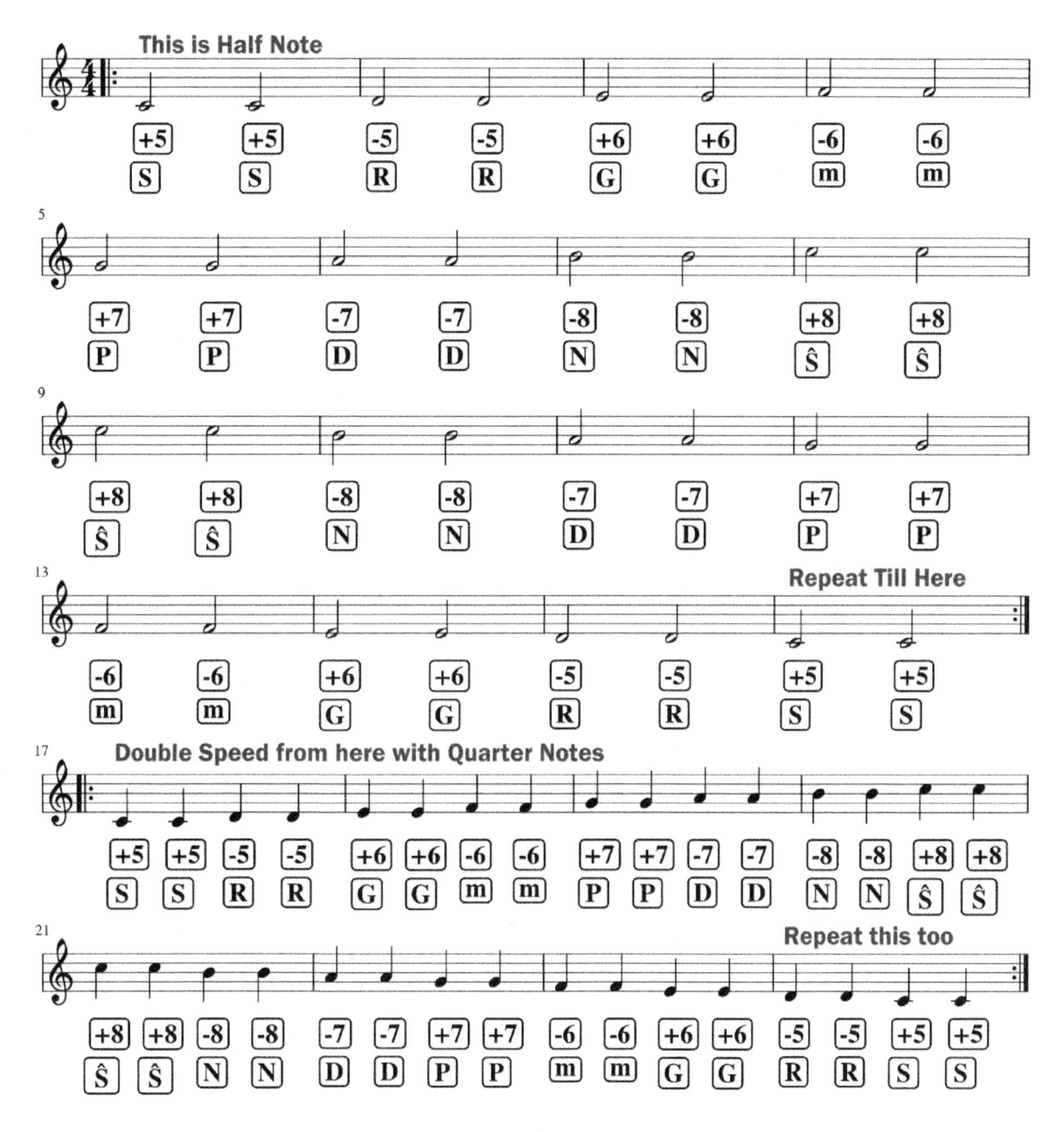

Lesson 3: Play 2 Same Notes at a time

5.3 Two sequential notes pattern

During this exercise, we will practice two sequential notes on each time signature with a slower tempo as previous one (60 – 80 BPM). Similar to the previous Sheet Music practice, the same notes are created in Half

(1/2) notes from 1-16 measures and on Quarter (1/4) notes from 17-24 measures. This will give confidence to the learner to play at either Half note speed or at quarter note speed. Another reason, for two rhythms, is to make the learner comfortable at both Half & Quarter notes.

With this lesson, learner will learn to play a bit on higher octave & lower octave. See the measure number 8 contains the notes R̂Ŝ (in western DC). Similarly 16th measure contains N̠S. Same notes are followed in the quarter notes too.

Playing 2 Sequencial Notes

- Harmonica Tabs
- Indian notes
- by Riddhi Sanyal

This is Half Note

+5	-5	-5	+6	+6	-6	-6	+7
S	R	R	G	G	m	m	P

+7	-7	-7	-8	-8	+8	-9	+8
P	D	D	N	N	Ŝ	R̂	Ŝ

+8	-8	-8	-7	-7	+7	+7	-6
Ŝ	N	N	D	D	P	P	m

Repeat Till Here

-6	+6	+6	-5	-5	+5	-4	+4
m	G	G	R	R	S	N̠	S

Double Speed from here with Quarter Notes

+5	-5	-5	+6	+6	-6	-6	+7	+7	-7	-7	-8	-8	+8	-9	+8
S	R	R	G	G	m	m	P	P	D	D	N	N	Ŝ	R̂	Ŝ

Repeat this too

+8	-8	-8	-7	-7	+7	+7	-6	-6	+6	+6	-5	-5	+5	-4	+4
Ŝ	N	N	D	D	P	P	m	m	G	G	R	R	S	N̠	S

Lesson 4: Play 2 Sequential Notes at a time

5.4 Play a pattern with skipping one note

The alternate notes like CE, DF, EG ... (Indian Notes: SG, Rm, GP ...) should be played and practiced. In this exercise, we will learn playing alternative notes at both upward & downward direction. Practicing more and more these exercises will orchestrate position of your Harmonica with your mind and it will gradually build reflex. Initially these exercises should be played with lower tempo. However, down the line once you are familiar, you can increase the tempo until you are comfortable. This notation will gradually increase the area of playing of your harmonica.

Play Alternative Notes with Skiping One Note
- Harmonica Tabs
- Indian notes
- by Riddhi Sanyal

This is Half Note

+5	+6	-5	-6	+6	+7	-6	-7
S	G	R	m	G	P	m	D

+7	-8	-7	+8	-8	-9	+10	+8
P	N	D	Ŝ	N	R̂	Ḡ	Ŝ

+8	-7	-8	+7	-7	-6	+7	+6
Ŝ	D	N	P	D	m	P	G

Repeat Till Here

-6	-5	+6	+4	-5	-4	-3	+4
m	R	G	S	R	N̠	D̠	S

Double Speed from here with Quarter Notes

+5	+6	-5	-6	+6	+7	-6	-7	+7	-8	-7	+8	-8	-9	+10	+8
S	G	R	m	G	P	m	D	P	N	D	Ŝ	N	R̂	Ḡ	Ŝ

Repeat this too

+8	-7	-8	+7	-7	-6	+7	+6	-6	-5	+6	+4	-5	-4	-3	+4
Ŝ	D	N	P	D	m	P	G	m	R	G	S	R	N̠	D̠	S

Lesson 5: Play Alternative Notes

5.5 Play simple notes to evolve into a Rhythm

This notation has been created to practice quarter and eighth notes in same measure. Another objective is to play in the same rhythm. Here we will use the quarter note and eighth note in the same way across all measures. The exercise follows simple 4+4 beats / Keherwa Taal. The notes are designed for the beginner with most of the consecutive notes to play. Practice as many times (ex: 30 times) in a session. The tempo can be slower as 60 – 80 BPM and set that in your metronome mobile app while playing this tune. Then after getting confidence, you can increase the tempo to 120 BPM.

Play Quarter & Eighth Notes in 4/4

- Harmonica Tabs
- Indian notes
- by Riddhi Sanyal

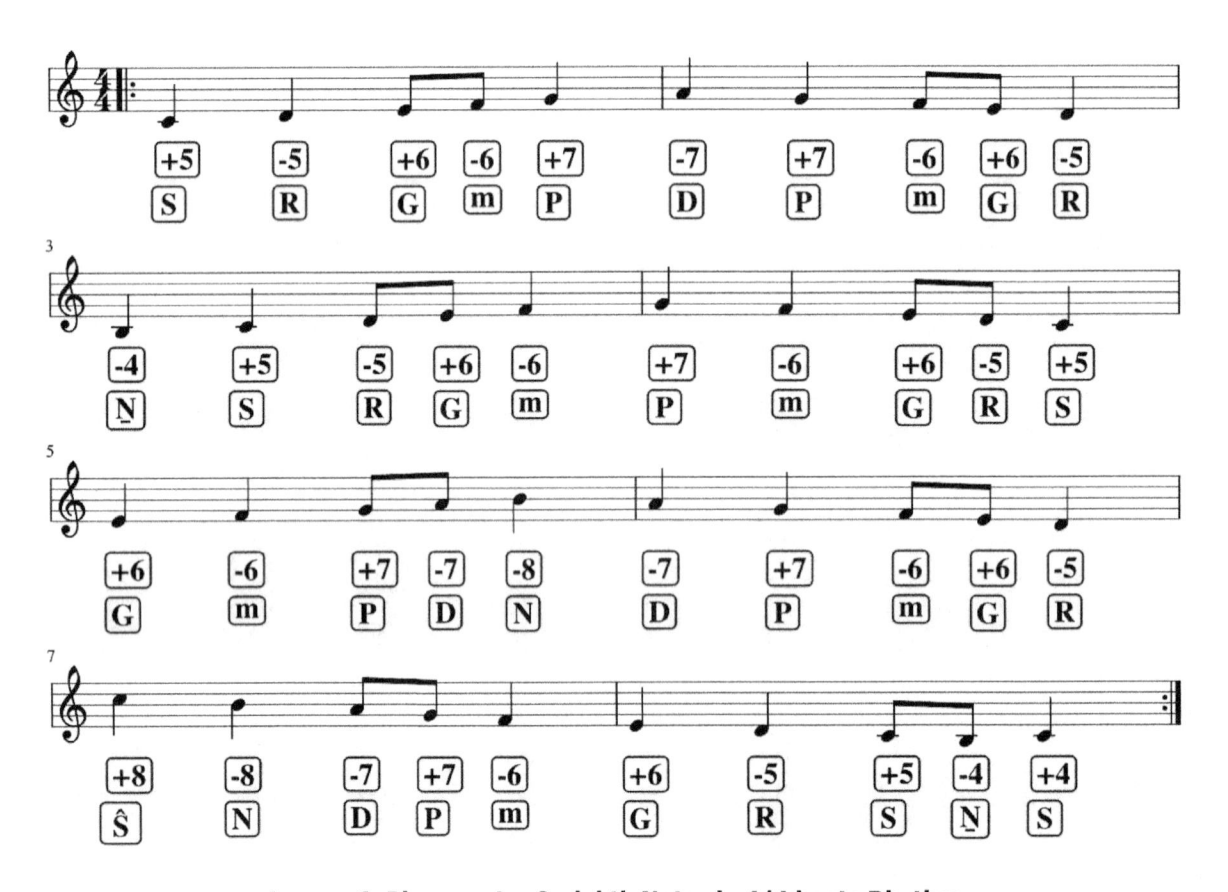

Measure 1-2: +5 -5 +6 -6 +7 | -7 +7 -6 +6 -5
S R G m P | D P m G R

Measure 3-4: -4 +5 -5 +6 -6 | +7 -6 +6 -5 +5
N S R G m | P m G R S

Measure 5-6: +6 -6 +7 -7 -8 | -7 +7 -6 +6 -5
G m P D N | D P m G R

Measure 7-8: +8 -8 -7 +7 -6 | +6 -5 +5 -4 +4
Ŝ N D P m | G R S N S

Lesson 6: Play quarter & eighth Notes in 4/4 beats Rhythm

5.6 Play three notes pattern

Playing 3 notes help in any stage of vocal / all instrumental practices. While playing in Harmonica, learner should always try to play in same tempo / rhythm. Higher octave notes and lower octave notes are also included in the practice. That will enrich the player to play beyond the octave. Set a lower tempo to start with (60). Once comfortable, you may increase the tempo without breaking it. You may need to exhale or breathe out between the measures 5th P **D N** and 6th **D N** Ŝ. But don't break the rhythm. You may feel the same while playing the descending measures in between 9th and 10th.

Sheet Music is created with 3/4 Tempo (3 beats in 1 measure). For better readability, 4 measures are given in 1 line. The notes are touching the Higher & Lower octave notes as well to give you complete practice with a rhythm.

Play 3 Note Pattern in 3/4 Rhythm
- Harmonica Tabs
- Indian notes
- by Riddhi Sanyal

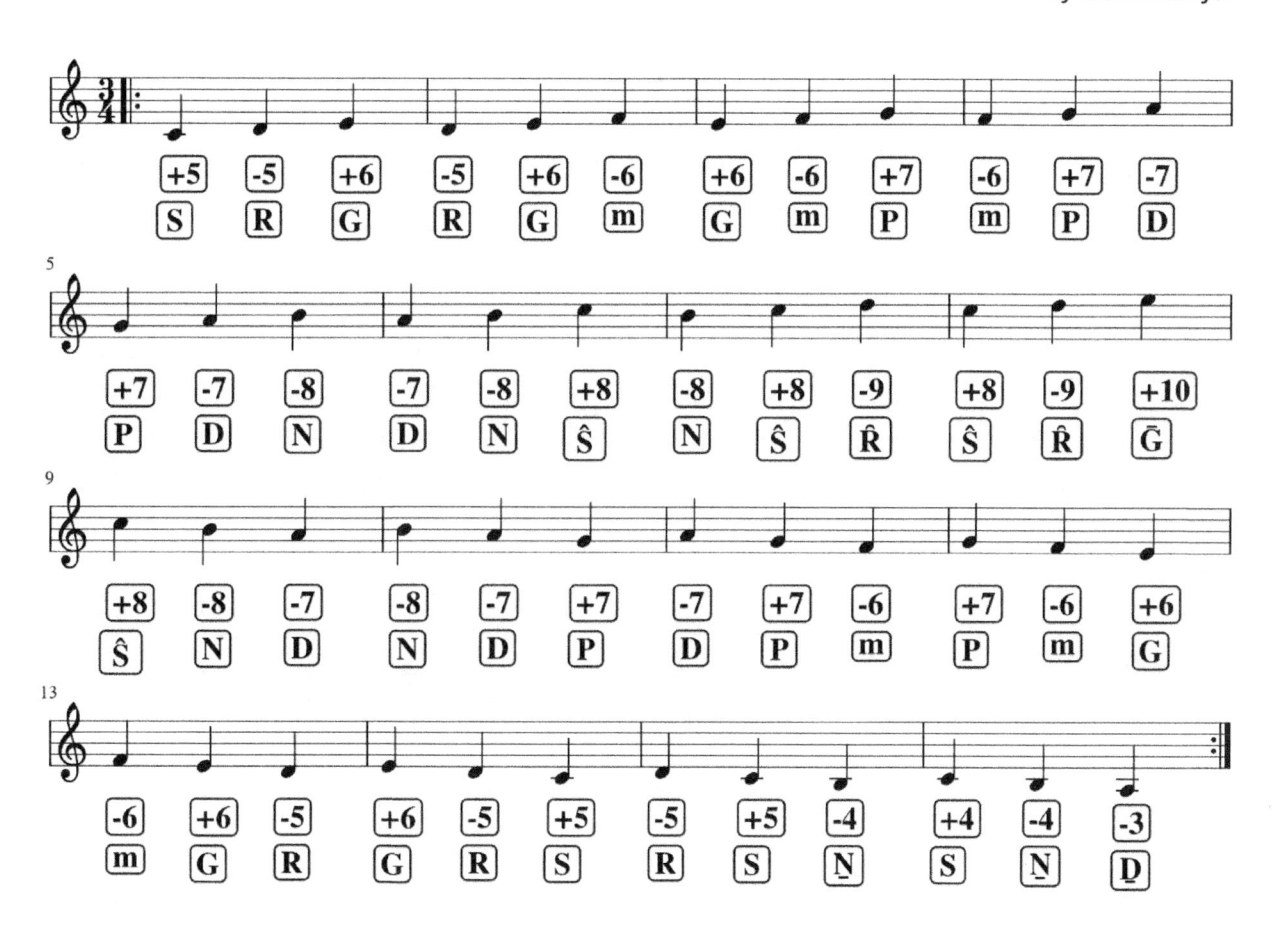

Line 1: +5 -5 +6 -5 +6 -6 +6 -6 +7 -6 +7 -7
S R G R G m G m P m P D

Line 2 (measure 5): +7 -7 -8 -7 -8 +8 -8 +8 -9 +8 -9 +10
P D N D N Ŝ N Ŝ R̂ Ŝ R̂ Ḡ

Line 3 (measure 9): +8 -8 -7 -8 -7 +7 -7 +7 -6 +7 -6 +6
Ŝ N D N D P D P m P m G

Line 4 (measure 13): -6 +6 -5 +6 -5 +5 -5 +5 -4 +4 -4 -3
m G R G R S R S N̲ S N̲ D̲

Lesson 7: Play Progression on 3 Notes in 6 beats (3/4)

5.7   Four Notes pattern

Similar to 3 notes, playing 4 notes is also very common in vocal or any instrumental practice. We have included lower and higher octave notes to improve learner's efficiency. Also the higher & lower octave notes forms nice filler music to accompany in the same rhythm. Most of the notes are consecutive notes and it will be easy to pick up. Sheet Music has the beating pattern … definitely 4/4. You can take your own tempo and try to increase with more practice. At one session, try to practice 30 – 40 times.

Play 4 Note Pattern in 4/4 Rhythm

- Harmonica Tabs
- Indian notes
- by Riddhi Sanyal

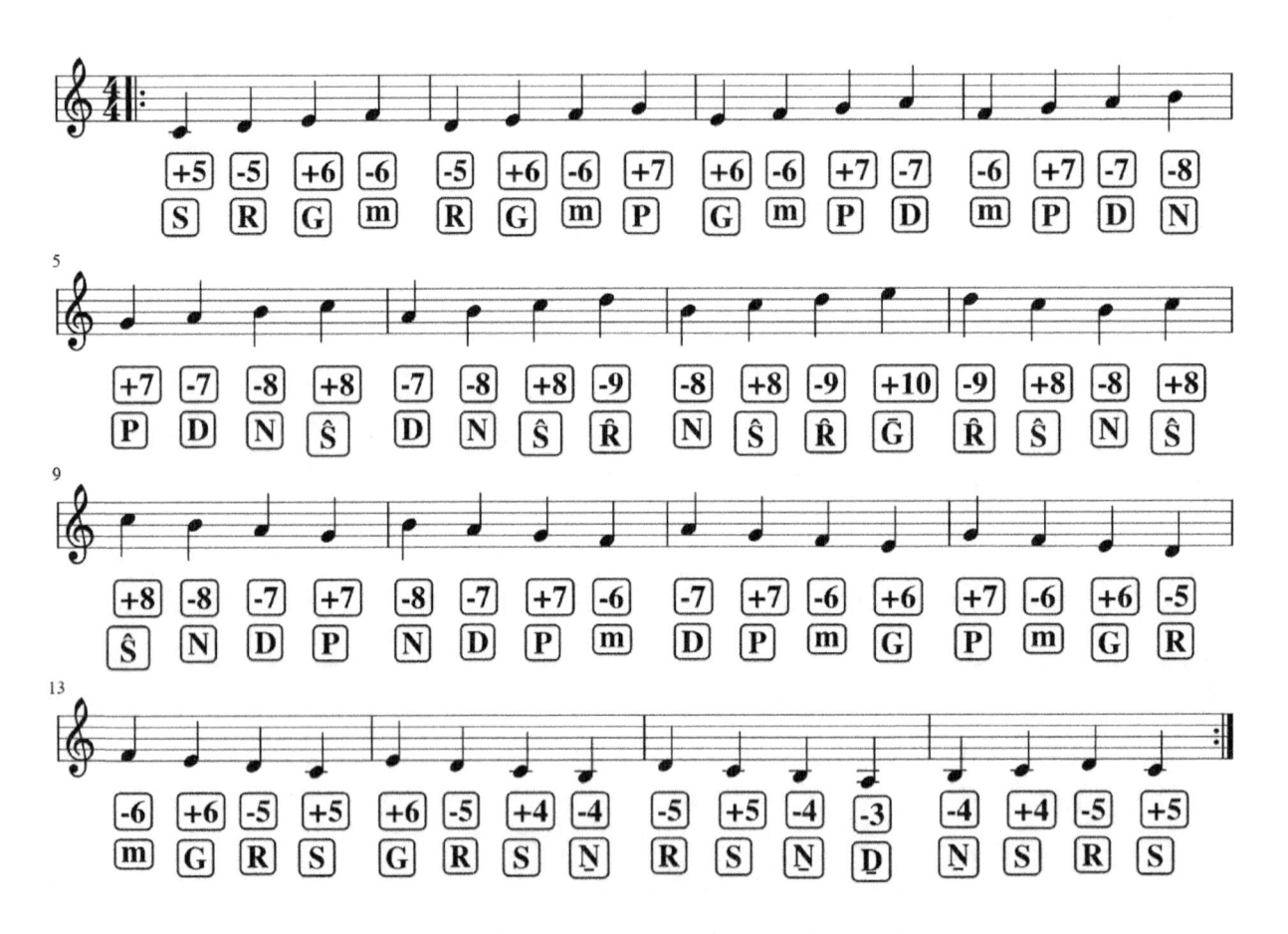

Lesson 8: Play Progression on 4 Notes in 8 beats (4/4)

5.8 Learn to play with Gaps

Once you are comfortable playing with beats, you should know the Rests/Gaps or silence.

This exercise we will start with whole Rest or Gap with whole note. Then next we will play with Half Note and Half Gaps. Slowly, we will move into quarter notes and Gaps. Finally we will play the Eighth notes and Eighth Gaps.

Starting from whole Notes & Gaps, then Half, Quarter and Eighth Gaps are represented in same sheet music gradually with self explanatory description. So you can understand that, the speed of the play will be changed 4 times, when we follow the notation.

Play Gaps Pattern in 4/4 Rhythm

- Harmonica Tabs
- Indian notes
- by Riddhi Sanyal

Whole Note with Gaps

+5 / S   (rest)   -5 / R   +6 / G

+7 / P   (rest)   -6 / m   +6 / G

Half Note with Gaps

+5 / S   -5 / R   +6 / G   +7 / P   -6 / m   +6 / G

Quarter Notes with Gaps

+5 / S   -5 / R   +6 / G   +7 / P   -6 / m   +6 / G   -5 / R   +6 / G   -6 / m   +7 / P   +7 / P

-7 / D   +7 / P   -6 / m   -5 / R   +6 / G   -6 / m   +7 / P   -6 / m   +6 / G   -5 / R   +5 / S   +5 / S

Eighth Notes with Gaps

+5 / S   -5 / R   +6 / G   +7 / P   -6 / m   +6 / G   -5 / R   +6 / G   -6 / m   +7 / P   +7 / P

-7 / D   +7 / P   -6 / m   -5 / R   +6 / G   -6 / m   +7 / P   -6 / m   +6 / G   -5 / R   +5 / S   +5 / S

Lesson 9: Learn Rest / Gap for Whole, Half, Quarter and Eighth Gaps

5.9 Have more control on Quarter & Eighth Notes with Gaps

This composition has been explicitly created to have more idea on the Notes & Rests in Quarter & Eighth note combinations. Once you can play this, you can easily pickup most of the songs as this notation will guide to stop for eighth gap as well as quarter gap.

Each line is set with repeat as well as whole notation should be repeated as illustrated with "D. C." symbol.

The tempo should be chosen in the same way. Initially choose very slow tempo like 60 – 80 BPM. Gradually increase and reach 120 BPM. Try to practice at least 30 – 40 times in one session and so that you can increase the tempo after every 10th practice.

Feel free to use +4 or +5 for the middle octave S (Sa) / C Note.

Play Quarter & Eighth Notes & Gaps
4/4 Rhythm

- Harmonica Tabs
- Indian notes
- by Riddhi Sanyal

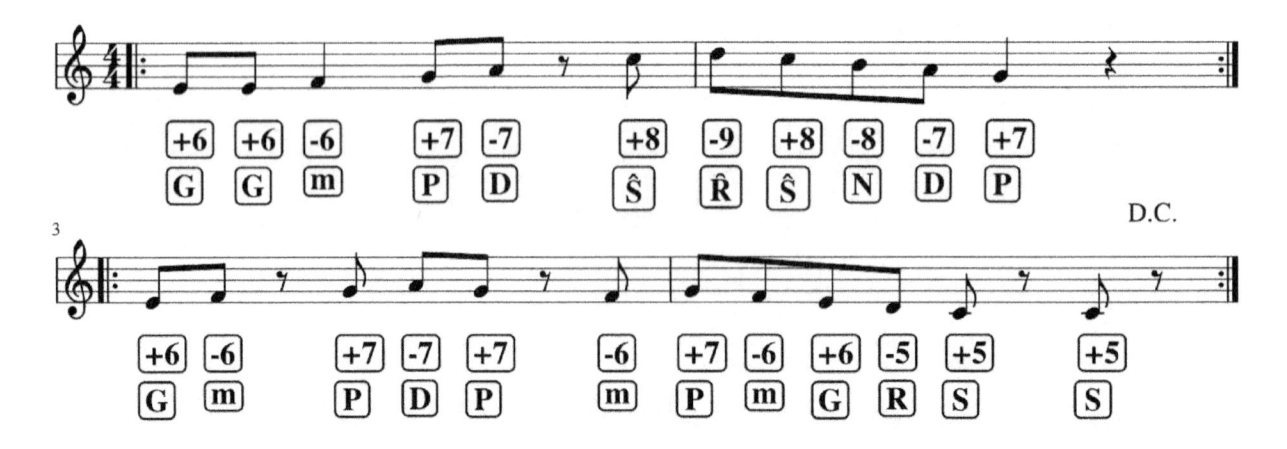

+6	+6	-6		+7	-7		+8	-9	+8	-8	-7	+7	
G	G	m		P	D		Ŝ	R̂	Ŝ	N	D	P	

D.C.

+6	-6		+7	-7	+7		-6	+7	-6	+6	-5	+5		+5	
G	m		P	D	P		m	P	m	G	R	S		S	

Lesson 10: Play Quarter & Eighth Notes & Rests (4/4)

5.10 Further Practices:

We are at the end of our lessons of preliminary lessons. For the benefit of students, few more patterns are given below. These will help to build the reflex more on the mouth position, hand movement and breathing.

> **Unique Four Beat Pattern**

As you are now comfortable on the 3 and 4 beat patterns, it's time to practice little bit different. During this exercise, you will play like the below 4 beat pattern. Follow the 4/4 beat metronome and play in a single tempo.

Ascending: **SGRS | RmGR | GPmG | mDPm | PNDP | DŜND | NR̂ŜN | ŜĜR̂Ŝ**

Descending: **ŜDNŜ | NPDN | DmPD | PGmP | mRGm | GSRG | RṈSR | SḎṈS**

Converting into C Scale notes, this becomes

Ascending: **CEDC | DFED | EGFE | FAGF | GBAG | AĈBA | BḊĈB | ĈĒḊĈ**

Descending: **ĈABĈ | BGAB | AFGA | GEFG | FDEF | ECDE | DḆCD | CA̱ḆC**

This particular practice will be easy to carry in Harmonica. Because the first phrase of each 4 notes, (Ex: SG ~ CE) is in same way of exhale. Similarly, next phrase, Rm (DF) is to draw air and so on except the area of PNDP (GBAG) and DŜND (AĈBA), but there also you will get 2 notes to inhale.

> **Unique Eight Beat Pattern**

This one is one more improvisation on the previous one. So first practice the 4 beat and then attempt this one. Even you can attempt this after the beginners' lessons too. Here we will add one more 4 beat into the last pattern and make this 8 beat pattern. Follow the 4 beat or 8 beat metronomes and play in a single tempo.

Ascending: **SGRS NSRS | RmGR SRGR | GPmG RGmG | mDPm GmPm …**

Descending: **ŜDNŜ R̂ŜNŜ | NPDN ŜNDN | DmPD NDPD | PGmP DPmP …**

Converting into C Scale notes, this becomes

Ascending: **CEDC ḆCDC | DFED CDED | EGFE DEFE | FAGF EFGF …**

Descending: **ĈABĈ ḊĈBĈ | BGAB ĈBAB | AFGA BAGA | GEFG AGFG …**

Here is a catch, I have written only the first 4 phrases of the notation. Please complete this notation in your handbook till the full octave like the previous one and then play.

6.0   Beginners Tunes and Songs on Harmonica

Till the previous exercises, you have already the confidence to play simple 3/4 and 4/4 beat pattern. Gradually we will play simple tune and songs. The songs are chosen in the best way to help you to learn them and gain the stability on Harmonica sounds. It will help you to memorize the position of notes in Harmonica and finally you will attain the reflex / memory on each notes of Harmonica, whether it's draw or blow with the exact Harmonica position. I believe that's our primary objective to help you on Harmonica.

Learning Period for the Beginners Lessons:

- This section will take approximately 20 – 30 days of your days of practice assuming you can pick up one song within 2 - 3 days.
- You should complete the further learning section of 5 more songs within 10 – 15 days. Please write the remaining notes of Further learning section at your comfortable notation.
- At max, if you sincerely practice daily, you can play the tunes and songs within 2 months.

These learning's are listed in the summary table for 10 selected Beginner songs.

SL	Name	Genre / Pattern	Rhythm	Taal	Tempo	Level	Learning On Harmonica
1	Twinkle Twinkle Little Star	Children's Music	4/4	Keherwa	Slow. Ex: 80 BPM	Beginner	• Learn to play with Taal. • Keep same Tempo. • Pause for Gaps
2	Wheels on the bus go round and round	Children's Music	4/4	Keherwa	Medium. Ex: 120 BPM	Beginner	• Play two notes and single notes in same verse • To get habituated in Sheet Music or Harmonica Tab Notes
3	Happy Birthday Tune	Children's Music / Traditional Folk	3/4 or 4/4	Dadra or Keherwa	Medium. Ex: 120 BPM	Beginner	• Better idea on Notes & Gaps • Once playing on both 3/4 and 4/4, we will learn the number of Gaps. • Learn minor Note Bb
4	Row Row Row your boat	Children's Music	3/4 or 4/4	Dadra or Keherwa	Slow. Ex: 80 - 100 BPM	Beginner	• Learn to play Triplets notes. • Key change and play entire tune in C#
5	O McDonald had a Farm	Children's Music	2/4 or 4/4	Keherwa	Medium. Ex: 120 BPM	Beginner	• Half, quarter and eighth notes are present as well as with gaps. • Rhythmic song • Play 2 notes together to build simple chords.
6	We Shall Overcome	Gospel Song	4/4	Keherwa	Slow	Beginner	• Stretch long notes with long breath. • Soft rhythm and beating pattern is unique • Melodious tune, repeat as many times you like
7	Jingle Bells	Christmas Carol	4/4	Keherwa	Slow. Ex: 80 - 100 BPM	Beginner	• Learn to play the Rhythmic song • Follow the beating style to play quarter & eighth (1/8) beats correctly.
8	Do A Deer	Show Tune	4/4	Keherwa	Slow	Beginner	• Musical & rhythmic tune • Unique rhythm with frequent note & pause.
9	Sholay – Harmonica Tune	Country, Satire	-	N.A.	Slow	Beginner	• Play with Vibration to generate the feel.
10	Simple Tune on Deshkar	Country Music	4/4	Keherwa	Medium. Ex: 120 BPM	Beginner	• Idea on Indian Raga Deshkar or Bhupali with 5 note out of 7 notes. Ex: S R G P D Ŝ.

Table 7: Simple Tunes for Beginners with the summary on the learning

6.1 Twinkle Twinkle Little Star

This is a simplest and well known tune across kids, adult and everyone. This is quite simple to play. So let's start this tune so that any learner can play them by heart. Please play at your comfortable tempo.

This tune has single note in a beat for most of the verses. Except, for the case where **two notes are in a single beat** and that is present at the verse "Up **above** the world so high".

About the Notation:

Learn "Twinkle Twinkle" in Sheet Music from the below sheet music. It's in standard 4/4 beats. To repeat the first line, D.C al Fine and Segno symbol is used. In the sheet music, **the gaps are replaced with the 1/2 note to end the lines**. For that, you need to hold the breath a bit more to play the 1/2 note.

We all know that it has 4 lines. This simple verse will help you to understand the sheet music if you don't have prior experience in music. See for repeat, at the end we have used "D. C. al Fine" at the last line, 8th measure. Also we can see that there is a "Fine" at the 2nd line or 4th measure. The code "D. C. al Fine" means, we have to repeat from start and play until "Fine" to conclude.

Twinkle Twinkle

- Harmonica Tabs, Sheet Music, Indian Notes by Riddhi Sanyal

Twin	kle	Twin	kle	lit	tle	star	
+5	+5	+7	+7	-7	-7	+7	
S	S	P	P	D	D	P	Fine

How	I	won	der	what	you	are
-6	-6	+6	+6	-5	-5	+5
m	m	G	G	R	R	S

Up	a	bove	the	world	so	high	
+7	+7	-6	-6	+6	+6	-5	
P	P	m	m	G	G	R	D.C. al Fine

Like	a	dia	mond	in	the	sky
+7	+7	-6	-6	+6	+6	-5
P	P	m	m	G	G	R

Lesson 11: Play 'Twinkle Twinkle'

6.2　　　Wheels on the bus go round and round

This is one of the popular songs for kids. This tune is so famous that everyone will like it. The notation of this is simple for Harmonica when **we start from Lower Pa** (G w.r.t. C). That will make all of the notes into the major notes in Harmonica.

The Lyrics of this song is given below for 3 verses –

Verses	Lyrics of the song
Para 1	The wheels on the bus go round and round Round and round Round and round The wheels on the bus go round and round All through the town
Para 2	The wipers on the bus go, "Swish, swish, swish" "Swish, swish, swish" "Swish, swish, swish" The wipers on the bus go, "Swish, swish, swish" All through the town
Para 3	The driver on the bus goes, "Move on back" "Move on back" "Move on back" The driver on the bus goes, "Move on back" All through the town

The Staff notation is prepared only for the first verse. The tune is same for all paragraphs. So you can easily play the tune for 3-4 times or as you wish.

About the Notes & Practice:

You might know this song already and you may able to play that. But it's really important to read the notation. So that it helps us to understand gradually. Some of the interesting things are –

- **Mostly it's 1/4 or quarter notes and 1/8 or eighth notes.**
- **First measure, the phrase "on the" has 1/8 notes.**
- **The Measures 3, 4 and 7 start with 1/4 Gap or Rests. Try to inhale or exhale as per need during this Rests.**
- **Measure 5 starts with 1/8 Gap or Rest. Then the first word "The" has 1/8 or eighth note.**

The Wheels on the Bus

*- Harmonica Tabs,
Sheet Music,
Indian Notes
by Riddhi Sanyal*

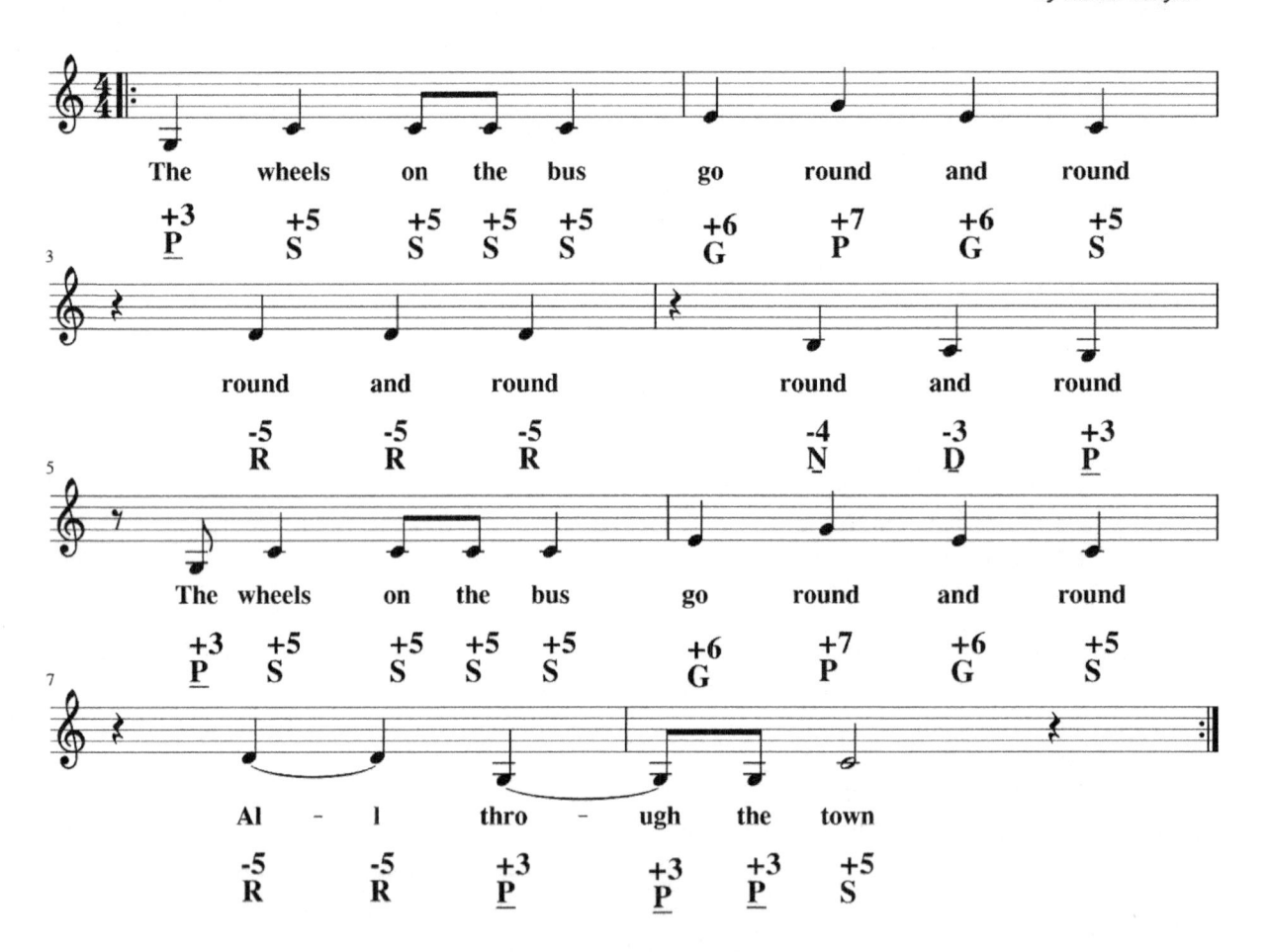

The	wheels	on	the	bus	go	round	and	round
+3	+5	+5	+5	+5	+6	+7	+6	+5
P	S	S	S	S	G	P	G	S

round	and	round		round	and	round
-5	-5	-5		-4	-3	+3
R	R	R		N	D	P

The	wheels	on	the	bus	go	round	and	round
+3	+5	+5	+5	+5	+6	+7	+6	+5
P	S	S	S	S	G	P	G	S

Al	-	l	thro	-	ugh	the	town
-5		-5	+3		+3	+3	+5
R		R	P		P	P	S

Lesson 12: The Wheels on the Bus

6.3 Happy Birthday Tune

Happy Birthday tune is one of the most popular tunes among any musicians in almost any instrument. We will start the tune from S (C). Here we will learn a new note – *Komal* / Flat ni (A# or Bb). Hence to proceed, we will first learn the minor note and then the HBD tune.

About the Notes & Practice: To play the **Komal ni (A# or Bb), we have to draw the air in the same place of Dha (A) with the "changer key" in pressed.** You can refer to the table earlier with all notes provided.

"Chromatic Harmonica - Blowing Positions with Notes on the Key of C".

This time, for Happy Birthday in western notation, we will follow 4/4 beat. Every line is ended with gaps. That will help you to pause for the desired gaps. Repeat symbol is given for entire notation. You can play for multiple times as you wish.

Play the HBD tune in any metronome app or beats app. Set 4 beats there and every beat, you should follow 1/4 notes in the Sheet music.

Happy Birthday to You

- Simplified Harmonica Notes by Riddhi Sanyal

Lyric	Hap	py	birth	day	to	you
Note	+5 S	+5 S	-5 R	+5 S	-6 m	+6 G

Lyric	Hap	py	birth	day	to	you
Note	+5 S	+5 S	-5 R	+5 S	+7 P	-6 m

Lyric	Hap	py	birth	day	dear	[Your	name]
Note	+5 S	+5 S	+8 Ŝ	-7 D	-6 m	+6 G	-5 R

Lyric	Hap	py	birth	day	to	you
Note	-7s n	-7s n	-7 D	-6 m	+7 P	-6 m

Lesson 13: Play Happy Birthday

Key Learning's from HBD:

- Better idea on Notes & Gaps.
- Once playing on both 3/4 and 4/4, we will learn the number of Gaps.
- Learn minor Note Bb.
- First word in each line is "Happy" which is coming as 1/8 + 1/8 beat. That except that, all other words is about 1/4 beat long. Once you play using metronome, you can realize this.

Further Study: Please note that, HBD can also be played starting from the lower octave Indian Note Pa (G w.r.t. C scale) without any flat or minor notes. Please start from lower Pa (G) and find the tune yourself. Write down the complete notation in your notebook and then play.

6.4 Row Row Row Your Boat

This is one of the simple songs and should be played in Harmonica. This will help you to play single, double and triple note in the simplest and smallest song. The song follows 4/4 beats pattern (8 Beat in Indian Taal like Dadra).

Verse of the song:

> Row, row, row your boat,
> Gently down the stream.
> Merrily, merrily, merrily, merrily,
> Life is but a dream.

About Notes & Practice and the learning's: We will start the song at C as like others. After repeating the song, we will play again with the Key On and shift to C# scale. All positions of the play will be same with Key on.

By this pattern of playing, you will realize that how the western songs can be played with half shifted scale (Ex: from, C → C#). So summarizing our learning through this wonderful song –

- **Learn 1/3 of a note. Ex: Each time on the phrase 'Merrily', we have to play the same note 3 times in 1/3 of the quarter note duration.**
- **Time Gap of consecutive notes may not be same. Ex: on the phrase 'row your', 2 eighth notes are used, but first one will be played for 1.5 time interval, and the 2nd eight note will be played for 0.5 time interval. Similar rhythmic phrases are used at all of the consecutive Eighth notes. For example –**
- **'Gent-ly'**
- **'down the'**
- **'Life is'**
- **'but a'**
- **Scale Changing: After playing the entire song twice, task is given for you to play the entire song again with pressing the Changer Key. That will simply guide you to experiment the same technique for other songs as well.**

Here is the combined Notation –

Row Row Row

*Simplified Sheet Music,
Harmonica Tabs,
Indian Notes,
by Riddhi Sanyal*

♩ = 100
Start at C

Row — row — row — your boat — Gent - ly down — the stream
+4 — +4 — +4 — -5 — +6 — +6 — -5 — +6 — -6 — +7
S — S — S — R — G — G — R — G — m — P

Mer-ri-ly mer-ri-ly mer-ri-ly mer-ri-ly Life is but a dream
+8 +8 +8 +7 +7 +7 +6 +6 +6 +4 +4 +4 +7 -6 +6 -5 +4
Ṡ Ṡ Ṡ P P P G G G S S S P m G R S

Start at C# - Key on for Harmonica

Row — row — row — your boat — Gent - ly down — the stream
+4s — +4s — +4s — -5s — -6 — -6 — -5s — -6 — -6s — +7s
r — r — r — g — m — m — g — m — M — d

Mer-ri-ly mer-ri-ly mer-ri-ly mer-ri-ly Life is but a dream
+8s +8s +8s +7s +7s +7s -6 -6 -6 +4s +4s +4s +7s -6s -6 -5s +4s
ř ř ř d d d m m m r r r d M m g r

Lesson 14: Row Row Row your Boat at C and C#

Playing this with multiple scales helps you to understand on how people shift the scales during a song.

6.5   Old MacDonald had a Farm – the famous Rhythmic tune

This is one of the most popular songs for Kids. This song has lot of similar verses. Kids love to sing this song in chorus.

About the song:

- Song Name: Old MacDonald Had a Farm
- Written: 1706 or earlier
- Published: 1706
- Recorded: 1925
- Songwriter(s):   Thomas d'Urfey (probably)
- Lyricist(s):   Frederick Thomas Nettlingham

About the Notes & Practice: Well, we are going to learn something interesting while playing this. It's a simple song. Most of you will already know the tune by heart. So only you need to maintain the rhythm first. Then slowly you need to add Harmonics during playing the verse "**Ee i ee i o**". **Actual notation of that is "E E D D C" in Indian Notation it's "G G R R S"**. We are going to introduce simple harmonic sounds with that in tune with the capability of Harmonica. **We will play "EC EC DB DB C"**. Same in **Indian notes looks like "GS GS RN RN S"**. Here EC (in Indian, GS) should be played together in single blow of Harmonica. Similarly DB (in Indian RN) should be played in single drawing of air through Harmonica. So that will give you the essence of chorus sound or harmonic sound. I am sure you will also love that.

We will only play this Harmonic trick during the verse "Ee i ee i o" to highlight that in the song. Rest of the song will be in normal single notes only.

Couple of verses are given. It has more than 5-6 verses with similar tune. You can play the song in Harmonica for 2-3 times or more when you perform.

Verses	Lyrics
Verse 1	Old MacDonald had a farm Ee i ee i o And on his farm he had some cows Ee i ee i oh With a moo-moo here And a moo-moo there Here a moo, there a moo Everywhere a moo-moo Old MacDonald had a farm Ee i ee i o
Verse 2	Old MacDonald had a farm Ee i ee i o And on his farm he had some chicks Ee i ee i o With a cluck-cluck here And a cluck-cluck there Here a cluck, there a cluck Everywhere a cluck-cluck Old MacDonald had a farm Ee i ee i o

Old MacDonald Had a Farm

- Simplified Notes in Staff Notes, Harmonica Tabs, Indian Notes by Riddhi Sanyal

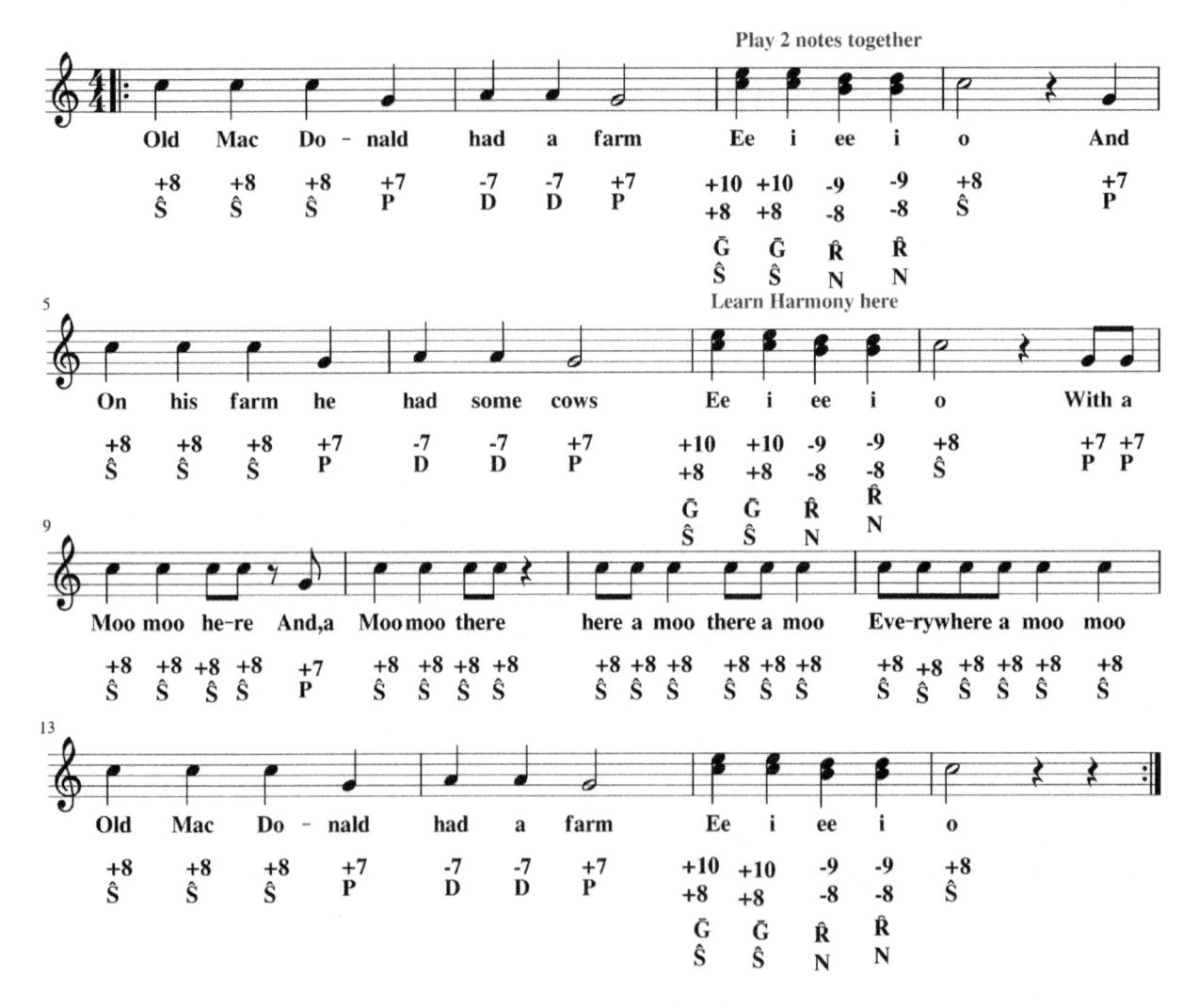

Play 2 notes together

Old	Mac	Do-nald	had	a	farm	Ee	i	ee	i	o		And
+8	+8	+8	+7	-7	-7	+7	+10	+10	-9	-9	+8	+7
Ŝ	Ŝ	Ŝ	P	D	D	P	+8	+8	-8	-8	Ŝ	P
							Ḡ	Ḡ	R̂	R̂		
							Ŝ	Ŝ	N	N		

Learn Harmony here

On	his	farm	he	had	some	cows	Ee	i	ee	i	o	With a
+8	+8	+8	+7	-7	-7	+7	+10	+10	-9	-9	+8	+7 +7
Ŝ	Ŝ	Ŝ	P	D	D	P	+8	+8	-8	-8	Ŝ	P P
							Ḡ	Ḡ	R̂	R̂		
							Ŝ	Ŝ	N	N		

Moo moo he-re	And, a Moo moo there	here a moo there a moo	Eve-rywhere a moo moo
+8 +8 +8 +8 +7	+8 +8 +8 +8	+8 +8 +8 +8 +8 +8	+8 +8 +8 +8 +8 +8
Ŝ Ŝ Ŝ Ŝ P	Ŝ Ŝ Ŝ Ŝ	Ŝ Ŝ Ŝ Ŝ Ŝ Ŝ	Ŝ Ŝ Ŝ Ŝ Ŝ Ŝ

Old	Mac	Do-nald	had	a	farm	Ee	i	ee	i	o
+8	+8	+8	+7	-7	-7	+7	+10	+10	-9	-9	+8
Ŝ	Ŝ	Ŝ	P	D	D	P	+8	+8	-8	-8	Ŝ
							Ḡ	Ḡ	R̂	R̂	
							Ŝ	Ŝ	N	N	

Lesson 15: Old MacDonald Had a Farm

Learning's on Harmonica:

Even this is one of the simple children music, once you are able to play in Harmonica, you will realize a lot of new things. Such as –

- Half, quarter and eighth notes are present as well as with gaps.
- Rhythmic song
- Play 2 notes together to build simple chords like Harmony. For Example –
    - **C Chord can be harmonized with C & E Notes together while blowing**
    - **G Chord can be harmonized with B & D Notes together while drawing**.

6.6   We Shall Overcome

To play with confidence, another known tune is given for practice – We Shall Overcome. This song is there almost with every language. You can easily play this almost by yourself if you have followed till now.

About the Song:

- Title: We Shall Overcome
- First Published on: 1901
- Genre: Originated as Gospel Song, Folk, then used in labour movement & Civil Rights
- Artist: Pete Seeger & several others
- Taal: 4/4 or Keherwa
- Tempo: Slow

Lyrics:

Verses	We Shall Overcome - Lyrics
Para 1	We Shall Overcome, we shall overcome We shall overcome someday. Oh, deep in my heart, I do believe, We shall overcome someday.
Para 2	We are not afraid, we are not afraid, We are not afraid today. Oh, deep in my heart, I do believe, We shall overcome someday.
Para 3	We are not alone, we are not alone We are not alone today Oh, deep in my heart, I do believe, We are not alone today.

About the Notes & Practice: Practice for at-least 10 - 20 times. **The last note "EF", in Indian 'Gm', is kind of filler music and it may not hold any lyrics.** So it's optional to play that 'Gm'. At the end / last cycle, you should not play the last note 'Gm'. It's only kept for repeating the entire song.

Enjoy the song in Sheet Music. 4/4 beats are used as the song demands. The entire song is repeated using repeat symbol.

The song has several verses. They all sound the same. So from a musician perspective, while presenting, you can repeat the song for 2-3 times.

We Shall Overcome

Western Notation,
Harmonica Tabs,
Indian Notes
- by Riddhi Sanyal

Lesson 16: Play 'We Shall Overcome'

Key Learning's on Harmonica:

- You can stretch the long notes with long breath. That gives better feel in the song.
- Soft rhythm and beating pattern is unique and followed in all 4 lines.
- Melodious tune, repeat as many times you like.

6.7   Jingle Bells

What a fun to play the Jingle Bells in any instruments. For Harmonica, as with full of harmony, the song 'Jingle Bells' gets a different dimension. This is fully rhythmic song and you need to be familiar with quarter, eight beats to play it in the proper tempo.

About the Song:

- Title: Jingle Bells
- Published: September 16, 1857, by Oliver Ditson & Co., Boston
- Composer(s): James Lord Pierpont
- Lyricist(s): James Lord Pierpont
- Originally titled as "The One Horse Open Sleigh"
- Genre: Christmas Carol
- Rhythm or Taal: 4/4. Indian Taal is Keherwa.
- Tempo: Slow to medium.

Lyrics:

Song position	Lyrics
Phrase 1	Dashing through the snow
	In a one-horse open sleigh
	O'er the fields we go
	Laughing all the way.
	Bells on bob tail ring
	Making spirits bright
	What fun it is to ride and sing
	A sleighing song tonight! Oh!
Phrase 2	Jingle bells, jingle bells,
	Jingle all the way.
	Oh! what fun it is to ride
	In a one-horse open sleigh. Hey!
	Jingle bells, jingle bells,
	Jingle all the way;
	Oh! what fun it is to ride
	In a one-horse open sleigh.

About the Notes & Practice: Notes wise, all major notes are used if we start the song from lower Pa (G w.r.t. C scale). The English verse is given for reference. Most of you may already know that. If you know the verse, it will help you to give a position to pause or play 1/8 beat or 1/4 beat like that.

Key Learning's on Harmonica:

- Learn to play the Rhythmic song
- Follow the beating style to play quarter (1/4) & eighth (1/8) beats correctly.

➢ Couple of notes are of 1/16 length. Try to play that with short breath and maintain the Rhythm / Taal.

Jingle Bells

Western Notation,
Harmonica Tabs,
Indian Notes
- by Riddhi Sanyal

♩ = 100
4/4

Dash - ing thru' the snow   In a one horse op - en sleigh
+3 +6 -5 +4 +3   +3 +3 +3 +6 -5 +4 -3
P G R S P   P P P G R S D

O'er the fields we go   Laugh - ing all the way
-3 -6 +6 -5 -4   +7 +7 -6 -5 +6
D m G R N   P P m R G

Bells on bob tail ring   Ma - king spi - rit bright
+3 +6 -5 +4 +3   +3 +6 -5 +4 -3
P G R S P   P G R S D

What fun is to ride and sing   A sligh - ing song to - night Oh!
-3 -6 +6 -5 +7 +7 +7   +7 -7 +7 +6 -5 +5 +7
D m G R P P P   P D P G R S P

Jin - gle bells   Jin - gle bells   Jin - gle all the way
+6 +6 +6   +6 +6 +6   +6 +7 +5 -5 +6
G G G   G G G   G P S R G

Oh What fun it is to ride   In a one horse open sleigh Hey!
-6 -6 -6 -6 -6 +6 +6   +6 +6 -5 -5 +6 -5 +7
m m m m m G G   G G R R G R P

[2.] a one horse open sleigh
+7 +7 +6 -5 +4
P P G R S

Lesson 17: Jingle Bells

6.8 Do-A-Deer – The tune from Sound of Music

Well Sound of music is one of the best musical movies. The songs are really beautiful in both musical and with most simple rhythm. Because of simplicity, we should learn the songs for vocal or any instrumental practice. The most popular song "Do A Deer" depicts the creation of music, apply lyrics starting from learning the Octave / SARGAM.

About the Song:

- Title: Do-Re-Mi / Do A Deer A Female Deer
- Released: 1959
- Movie: The Sound of Music
- Genre: Show tune
- Composer(s): Richard Rodgers
- Lyricist(s): Oscar Hammerstein II
- Rhythm / Taal: 4/4 or Keherwa Taal
- Tempo: Slow to medium

External Links for original Song, Lyrics / Credits:

- To listen to the original video, please visit "Do-Re-Mi" - THE SOUND OF MUSIC (1965) on YouTube, Rodgers and Hammerstein
- To view the lyrics, you can visit - https://genius.com/Julie-andrews-do-re-mi-lyrics

About the Notes & Practice: Portion of the song is illustrated here the Indian notations, Harmonica Tabs and Staff Notation. Let us select these 3 verses to practice and play. Though it's 4/4 rhythm, but you will feel the different patterns of rhythm created in following 3 verses. At the end, you should repeat the first verse again as explained in the *Repeats* of the lyrics table.

Key Learning's:

- Learn 1/4, 1/8, as well as 1/2 and whole notes.
- Musical & rhythmic tune.
- Unique rhythm with frequent note & pause.

Do A Deer, A Female Deer

Simplified Notes in Harmonica Tabs, Indian Notes
- by Riddhi Sanyal

Do A Deer -->

+5	-5	+6	+6	+5	+6	+5	+6	+6	-5	+6	-6	-6	+6	-5	-6
S	R	G	G	S	G	S	G	G	R	G	m	m	G	R	m

+6	-6	+7	+6	+7	+6	+7	-6	+7	-7	-7	+7	-6	-7
G	m	P	G	P	G	P	m	P	D	D	P	m	D

+7	+5	-5	+6	-6	+7	-7	-7	-5	+6	-6	+7	-7	-8
P	S	R	G	m	P	D	D	R	G	m	P	D	N

Fine

-8	+6	-6	+7	-7	-8	+8	+8	-8	-7	-6	-8	+7	+8	+7	+6	-5
N	G	m	P	D	N	Ŝ	Ŝ	N	D	m	N	P	Ŝ	P	G	R

Do Mi Mi -->

+5	+6	+6	+6	+7	+7	-5	-6	-6	-7	-8	-8
S	G	G	G	P	P	R	m	m	D	N	N

So Do La ... -->

+7	+5	-7	-6	+6	+5	-5
P	S	D	m	G	S	R

+7	+5	-7	-8	+8	-9	+8
P	S	D	N	Ŝ	R̂	Ŝ

+7	+5	-7	-6	+6	+5	-5
P	S	D	m	G	S	R

D.S. al Fine

+7	+5	-7	-8	+8	-9	+8
P	S	D	N	Ŝ	R̂	Ŝ

Lesson 18: Do-A-Deer / Do-Re-Mi

6.9 Sholay – Harmonica Theme Tune

One of the best Harmonica tune in Bollywood songs was given by our Legend R. D. Burman on the famous movie Sholay.

About the Tune:

- Title: **Sholay Harmonica Tune**
- Movie: **Sholay (1975)**
- Composer: **Rahul Dev Burman**
- Cast for this Tune: **Amitabh Bachan**

About the Notes & Practice: This tune is easy to learn, but to get the feel is difficult. This tune is not actually in any Taal or Rhythm. Still a tempo has been considered in western notes as 160 to give the feel. It was originally with the soft guitar chords. Once you learn the tune, feel free to stay more time on any notes or give more gaps. Only need is to create the feeling on the tune. Apply vibration with wind where you have to sustain for long. Vibration symbol is given on the Staff Notes.

Sholay - Harmonica Tune
The famous tune from Sholay

- Simplified Staff Notes in C Major & Harmonica Tab Notes by Riddhi Sanyal

♩ = 160

| +5 | -5 | +6 | -7 | -7 | | +6 | -7 | +6 | +6 | +6 |
| S | R | G | D | D | | G | D | G | G | G |

| +5 | -5 | +6 | -7 | -7 | | +6 | -7 | -5 | -5 | -5 |
| S | R | G | D | D | | G | D | R | R | R |

| -6 | | -6 | +6 | -5 | -5 | +5 | -5 | -6 | -5 | -4 | -4 |
| m | | m | G | R | R | S | R | m | R | N | N |

| -4 | +4 | -5 | +6 | -6s | +7 | -7 | -8 | -6 | +7 | -6 | +6 | +6 | +6 |
| N | S | R | G | M | P | D | N | m | P | m | G | G | G |

Lesson 19: Sholay Harmonica Tune

6.10   Simple Tune on *Deshkar* – by Guruji Sri D Madhusudan

The beauty of Guruji, Sri D. Madhusudan, is on his compositions. With multi-instrumental capabilities, he has created the composition for all musicians like Guitar, Mandolin, Flute, Violin, Harmonica, Banjo, Sarod, Piano etc. During this composition, we will learn a *Dhun* on Raga Deshkar on Western pattern 4/4 beats. The notes are too touchy and follow Raga *Deshkar*, but it's westernized. It's ideal to play in the instruments like Violin, Harmonica, and Piano etc. The students of Guruji earlier played that on one of the annual function with Group of Violins.

About the composition:

- **Name: Simple Tune on Deshkar**
- **Composer: Guruji Sri D. Madhusudan**
- **Year of Publication: 2015**
- **First Performed by: Beniyasahakala on 2016 Annual Function**
- **Beating Pattern: 4/4 or Keherwa Taal.**
- **Style of Music: This tune follows Indian Classical Raga *Deshkar*, but westernized for Group performance.**

About the Notes & Practice: The tune uses only 5 Major notes – S R G P D according to the Raga. The Deshkar Raga gives more priority on the note D than G. That differentiates the Raga Deshkar from the Raga Bhupali. No Minor notes are used.

Verses: This music composition has no words and it's only for musicians. It has 3 verses – Bandish, Antara 1 and Antara 2.

Key Learning's on Harmonica:

- Idea on Indian Raga Deshkar or Bhupali with 5 notes out of 7 notes. Ex: S R G P D Ṡ.
- Learn Antara with different tunes as here Antara 1 and Antara 2 are different.
- This Tune is ideal for Group performances. If you have anyone to accompany, you can play and perform in a Group.

Simple Tune on Deshkar

Guruji Sri D. Madhusudan

- Harmonica Notes
Maintained Originality
- by Riddhi Sanyal

♩ = 120

Bandish

| +5 | +5 | -5 | +5 | +7 | -7 | +7 | -7 | +7 | -7 | +7 | +5 | -5 | +6 |
| S | S | R | S | P | D | P | D | P | D | P | S | R | G |

| +7 | -7 | +7 | -5 | +7 | -7 | +7 | +6 | +7 | -7 | +8 | +7 | -7 | +7 |
| P | D | P | R | P | D | P | G | P | D | Ŝ | P | D | P |

To Coda — Fine — D.S. al Coda

| -5 | +6 | -5 | +7 | +6 | -5 | +5 |
| R | G | R | P | G | R | S |

Antara 1

| +5 | -5 | +6 | -5 | +7 | +7 | +6 | -5 | +6 | -5 | +5 | +7 |
| S | R | G | R | P | P | G | R | G | R | S | P |

| +6 | +7 | +6 | +5 | -7 | -7 | -5 | +6 | +7 | +6 | -5 | +5 |
| G | P | G | S | D | D | R | G | P | G | R | S |

| +7 | -7 | +8 | +7 | -7 | +7 | +7 | -7 | -9 | +10 | -9 | +8 |
| P | D | Ŝ | P | D | P | P | D | R̂ | Ḡ | R̂ | Ŝ |

D.S. al Coda

| -7 | +7 | -7 | +7 | -5 | +6 | +7 | -7 | +7 | -7 | +7 | +6 | -5 | +5 |
| D | P | D | P | R | G | P | D | P | D | P | G | R | S |

Antara 2

| +6 | -5 | +5 | +7 | +6 | -5 | +5 | +7 | -7 | +8 | +7 | -7 | -9 | +8 |
| G | R | S | P | G | R | S | P | D | Ŝ | P | D | R̂ | Ŝ |

| -7 | +7 | -5 | +6 | -7 | +7 | +6 | +6 | +7 | +8 | -7 | +6 | -5 | +6 |
| D | P | R | G | D | P | G | G | P | Ŝ | D | G | R | G |

[Musical notation: Lesson 35, marked "D.S. al Fine"]

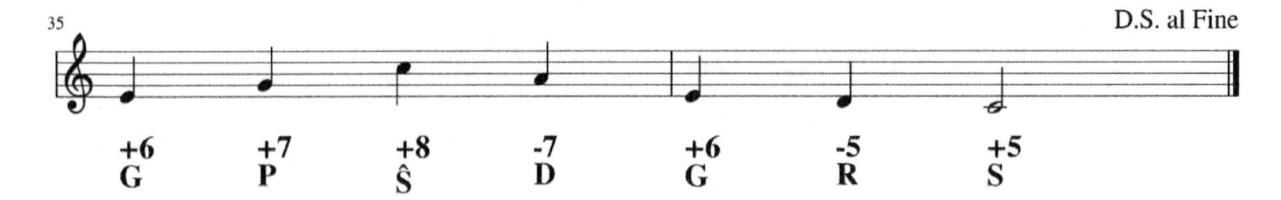

```
+6   +7   +8   -7   +6   -5   +5
 G    P    Ŝ    D    G    R    S
```

Lesson 20: Simple Tune in Deshkar

6.11   Further Learning

There are some more songs for you to explore on your own. We have listed few beginner level songs which you can try now.

> **Silent night, Holy night**

This is one of the peaceful melodies on the Christmas carol songs. Thought created, 200 years back, the tune is still popular. This was created in German in composed in 1818 by Franz Xaver Gruber. Later, this one was translated in English. This is in slow 6/8 rhythm or Indian Taal Dadra. You can start this tune like –

Indian Notes:

"P – DP | G – – | P – DP | G – – |"

"R̂ – – | N – – | Ŝ – – | P – – |"…

Western Notes:

"G – AG | E – – | G – AG | E – –|

"Ḋ – – | B – – | Ĉ – – | G – – |"…

You can get more details on Silent Night from https://en.wikipedia.org/wiki/Silent_Night

> **Ode to Joy, from Symphony No 9, by Beethoven**

Needless to say that most of us has heard this tune from childhood. If you are new to this tune, you should listen the tune first in YouTube or any Music Station. The Sheet Music of "Ode To Joy" is already present in the Wikipedia site given below and it's available in the section named "**IV. Finale**". That notation is on 4/4. You can start like this –

Indian Notes:

"G G m P | P m G R | S S R G | G S S – |"…

Western Notes:

"E E F G | G F E D | C C D E | E C C – |"…

> **Lakdi Ki Kaathi**

Song Name: Lakdi Ki Kaathi, Movie: Masoom Singers: Gauri Bapat, Gurpreet Kaur, Vanita Mishra, Lyrics: Gulzar Music: R. D. Burman, Music Label: Shemaroo. This is one of the most popular Kid's songs in India from Bollywood movies. This can be played on 2/4 or 4/4 beats or Indian Taal Keherwa.

You can simply start like –

Indian Notes:

"S S R G | P – G R | S S R G | P – G R | S S R G | P – G R | S S R G | P – P – |"…

Western Notes:

"C C D E | G – E D | C C D E | G – E D | C C D E | G – E D | C C D E | G – G – |"…

After playing the full song, you will definitely enjoy the tune and rhythm.

> **Jesus loves the little children**

This is one of the famous children prayer songs. The words were written by preacher Clarence Herbert Woolston (1856–1927). It has only 4 verses to remember. The tune is simple and truly nice in Harmonica or any western instruments.

You can start this like –

Indian Notes:

"| Ĝ – Ĝ – | Ĝ R̂ Ŝ D | P – Ŝ – | R̂ – R̂ – | Ĝ R̂ Ŝ Ĝ |

| R̂ – – Pm | G P Ŝ R̂ | Ŝ – Ŝ N | D N Ŝ D | P – "…

Western Notes:

"| Ē – Ē – | Ē Ḋ Ĉ A | G – Ĉ – | Ḋ – Ḋ – | Ē Ḋ Ĉ Ē |

| Ḋ – – G F | E G Ĉ Ḋ | Ĉ – Ĉ B | A B Ĉ A | G – "…

You can refer to this for further details - https://en.wikipedia.org/wiki/Christian_child%27s_prayer#Jesus_Loves_the_Little_Children

> **Imagine (John Lennon song)**

Released: 1971, Movie: Mr. Holland's Opus, Artist: John Lennon, Genres: Pop music, Soft rock, Alternative/Indie, Pop, Seasonal, Rock, and Folk.

Well this is one of the nice tune which you can quickly pickup in Harmonica. It's on soft rock 4/4 simple rhythm. This is how you can start –

Indian Notes:

"P P P NN | D – – DNS | P P P NN | D – – DNS | … | :D S D S | G G R – |"…

Western Notes:

"G G G BB | A – – ABC | G G G BB | A – – ABC | … | :A C A C | E E D – |"…

You will enjoy this soft rock / folk beats if you play with the karaoke music.

Please write all of these notations at your notepad and then play. Writing notation will help you to memorize the song at later point of time.

7.0 Intermediate Level Tunes for Harmonica

Once you complete all of the beginner lessons, you will be more confident on **Tune** & **Rhythm**. Now slowly, you can pick up the intermediate tunes. Every tune has been chosen here for a definite learning goal. So here you will get to learn practically with your practice rather the theory. The tunes are gradually organized to give you the most benefit out of that. This intermediate section will more cover on a bit rhythmic songs on 4/4, waltz rhythm, 1-2 minor notes, vibration on some notes, to play the sections of interlude or section of with chords pattern etc.

Learning Period for the Intermediate Lessons:

➢ This section will take approximately 15 – 30 days of your days of practice assuming you can pick up one song within 2 - 3 days.

➢ You should add on the further learning section of 5 more songs within 10 – 15 days.

➢ Overall, if you sincerely practice daily, you can play the tunes and songs within 2 - 3 months.

These learning's are listed in the summary table for 10 selected intermediate songs.

SL	Name	Genre / Pattern	Rhythm	Taal	Tempo	Level	Learning On Harmonica
1	A Chal Ke Tujhe	Indian Pop, Country	4/4	Keherwa	Slow	Beginner to Intermediate	• Play steadily with 4/4 simple rhythm • Minor note F# (Tibra Ma) is present along with F (normal ma).
2	Santa Lucia	Traditional Music, World Music	3/4 Waltz	Dadra	Slow	Beginner to Intermediate	• Learn to play with 3/4 waltz beats. • Minor note F# (Tibra Ma) is present along with F (normal ma).
3	Jamaican Farewell	Jamaican Folk Music / Mento	4/4	Keherwa	Medium. Ex: 120 BPM	Intermediate	• Learn to play with Off-Beat starting • Try Note bending when the sound lasts
4	Title Music	Indian Pop, Opening Ceremony Song, Happy Mood	4/4	Keherwa	Medium. Ex: 120 BPM	Intermediate	• Learn to play with Vibration • Try 2 notes together in chords fashion • Try to end differently, ex: ending with higher octave
5	O Sona Byang O Kola Byang	Children's Music, Touch of Raga Yaman Kalyan	6/4 or 3/4	Dadra	Fast, Ex: 160 - 240	Intermediate	• Learn to play with 3/4 or 6/4 beats • Minor note F# (Tibra Ma) is present along with F (normal ma). Nice experience to play both notes in same verse.

SL	Name	Genre / Pattern	Rhythm	Taal	Tempo	Level	Learning On Harmonica
6	Hai Apna Dil To Aawara	Indian Pop	4/4	Keherwa	Fast, Ex: 200	Intermediate	• Play chord like Harmony with two notes • Original famous interlude music is in Harmonica. • Learn Eb or Komal ga
7	Minuet	Traditional Music	3/4	Dadra	Medium	Intermediate	• Though it's a beginner for Piano, I will keep this in Intermediate in Harmonica for it's unique 3/4 rhythm. • Only Minor note is F# (Tibra Ma)
8	Pran Chay Chokkhu Na Chay	Bhairavi Baul, Folk Based, Tagore song	4/4	Tintaal (16 beats). nowadays played in Keherwa style	Fast	Intermediate	• Minor scale (Phrygian mode) or Raga Bhairavi based tune to be learned in the easiest way in harmonica with changing the starting note. In this case, the start of the song is from Dha or A w.r.t. C Scale. • Only Minor notes become Bb or n (Komal Ni) and F# or M (Tibra Ma)
9	500 Miles Away From Home	Country	4/4	Keherwa	Slow	Beginner to Intermediate	• Simple slow rhythm on 4/4 beats • This tune follows the Bhupali Raga with the notes - S R G P D Ṡ. So this will help us to practice the songs related to Bhupali Raga.
10	Music for Wind	Slow Rock, Waltz	3/4	Dadra	Slow	Intermediate	• Vibration or Note bending are the main factors to create the feel.

Table 8: Intermediate Level Tunes & summary on the learning

7.1 A Chal Ke Tujhe

We all love the song "A Chal Ke Tujhe" from legendary singer Kishore Kumar. Particularly, Kishore ji was the singer, writer and composer of this peaceful song. Even he was the actor to sing the song.

About the Song:

- ➢ Song: A Chal Ke Tujhe
- ➢ Film: Door Gagan Ki Chhaaon Mein
- ➢ Music Director: Kishore Kumar
- ➢ Lyricist: Kishore Kumar
- ➢ Singer(s): Kishore Kumar
- ➢ Taal or Rhythm: 4/4 or Keherwa taal with simple rhythmic style

- **Tempo: Slow**
- **Pattern / Genre: Indian Pop, Country.**

Minor Notes: Tibra Ma (M) or F# w.r.t. C scale. You can practice the minor note before playing this song by referring the **Table 2: Chromatic Harmonica - Blowing Positions**. For example, here to play this minor note, F#, you need to draw air at 6th Hole.

Learning From this Song:

- **Play steadily with 4/4 simple rhythm**
- **Minor note F# (Tibra Ma) is present along with F (normal ma).**

Lyrics:

Verses	Lyrics of the section
Bandish / Sthayi	Aa chal ke tujhe mein leke chalo Ek aise gagan ke tale Jaha ghum bhi na hon, asoon bhi na hon Bas pyar hi pyar pale Ik aise gagan ke tale
Antara 1	Suraj ki pehle kiran se aasha ka savera jaage Chanda ki kiran se dhulkar ghanghor andhera bhage (Kabhi dhoop khile, kabhi chaao mile Lambi si dagar na khale) →Tune similar to first line in Bandish Jaha ghum bhi na hon, asoon bhi na hon Bas pyar hi pyar pale
Antara 2	Jaha door nazar daudayem aazad gagan lehraye Jaha rang birange panchi asha ka sandesha laye (Sapno mein pali hasti ho kalim jaha shyam suhani dhale) →Tune similar to first line in Bandish Jaha ghum bhi na hon, asoon bhi na hon Bas pyar hi pyar pale
Antara 3	Sapno ke aise jahan mein jaha pyar hi pyar khila hon Hum jake waha kho jayein, shikwa na koi gila hon (Kahi bair na hon, koi gair na hon Sab milke yun chalte chale) →Tune similar to first line in Bandish Jaha ghum bhi na hon, asoon bhi na hon Bas pyar hi pyar pale

The tune of Antara 1, Antara 2 and Antara 3 are identical and hence one of the Antara has been converted into Staff Notation with Harmonica Tabs.

A Chal Ke Tujhe

Lyrics, Music, Acting, Singer All by Kishore Kumar

- Simplified Staff Notes & Harmonica Tab Notes by Riddhi Sanyal

𝄋 Bandish

A chal ke tu - jhe main le ke cha - lu E - k
Dhu - up khi - le kabhi cha - o mi - le lam

P S S R S P S S R S P P
+3 +4 +4 -5 +4 +3 +4 +4 -5 +4 +3 +3

ai - se ga - gan ke ta - le - e - e Ja - han
bi si da - gar na kha - le - e - e

S S R G m G m G R P P
+4 +4 -5 +6 -6 +6 -6 +6 -5 +3 +3

ghum bhi na ho Aa - su bhi na ho Ba - s

R R G R p R R G R S R
-5 -5 +6 -5 +3 -5 -5 +6 -5 +4 -5

py - a - r hi py - ar pale I - k

N N S P P m G P P
-4 -4 +4 +7 +7 -6 +6 +3 +3

|1. |2. Fine

ai - se ga - gan ke ta - le A le

S S R G m G S P S
+4 +4 -5 +6 -6 +6 +4 +3 +4

Antara 1

Su - u - raj ki - i pe - he - le ki - ran se A - a -

G P S S R G P P D P G G m
+6 +7 +4 +4 -5 +6 +7 +7 -7 +7 +6 +6 -6

Continue from Bandish with same tune, different lyrics. Check Lyrics table to know more...

Lesson 21: A Chal Ke Tujhe

7.2 Santa Lucia

In our childhood, we used to listen this tune in "Tom & Jerry show" or "Popeye the Sailor". Later I realized the true power of the tune. Because of simplicity of the tune, we can pick up this world famous tune quite easily.

About the song:

- *Title: Santa Lucia*
- *The Artist: Traditional Music*
- *Composed: 1849*

Info: Santa Lucia is a traditional Neapolitan song. It was transcribed by in Sweden Teodoro Cottrau (1827–1879) to Italian and published by the Cottrau firm, as a barcarolla, at Naples in 1849. Cottrau translated it from Neapolitan into Italian during the first stage of the Risorgimento, the first Neapolitan song to be given Italian lyrics. The transcriber, who is very often credited as its composer, was the son of the French-born Italian composer and collector of songs Guillaume Louis Cottrau (1797–1847).

Lyrics: There are total 5 verses. But for us in Harmonica, only the tune matters. So just for reference first 2 verses in Italian are given. English translation of the first verse is given.

Song Verses	Lyrics
Italian Lyrics (Verse 1):	(Sul mare luccica l'astro d'argento. Placida è l'onda, prospero èil vento.) x2 Venite all'agile barchetta mia, Santa Lucia! Santa Lucia! Venite all'agile barchetta mia, Santa Lucia! Santa Lucia!
English Translation (Verse 1)	(On the sea glitters the silver star Gentle the waves, favourable the winds.) x2 Come into my nimble little boat, Saint Lucy! Saint Lucy! Come into my nimble little boat, Saint Lucy! Saint Lucy!
Verse 2	Con questo zeffiro, così soave Oh! Com'è bello star su la nave! Su passaggieri, venite via! Santa Lucia! Santa Lucia!

Taal / Rhythm: The rhythm goes in 3/4 mode (like Indian Dadra Taal). Only trick is to play the quarter & eighth note in the rhythm. This song goes in slower tempo. Choose your own tempo. Play with the vibration in Harmonica so that the tune has a true feeling.

Minor Note: This song uses only one minor Note that is Tibra Ma (M) or F# w.r.t. C.

Key Learning's in Harmonica:

- **Learn to play with 3/4 waltz beats.**

➢ **Minor note F# (Tibra Ma) is present along with F (normal ma).**

Santa Lucia
Traditional Music

- Simplified Staff Notes & Harmonica Tab Notes by Riddhi Sanyal

Sul ma - re Lu - ci - a l'a - stro - d'ar - gen - to - o
+7 +7 +8 +8 -8 -8 -6 -6 -7 -7 +7 +7
P P Ŝ Ŝ N N m m D D P P

Pla - ci - dae lon - da pros - pero èil ven - to
+6 -7 +7 +7 -6s -6 -6 +6 -5 -7 +7
G D P P M   m m G R D P

Ve - ni - te all' - a - gile bar - che - tta mi - a - a
+10 -9 +8 -8 -7 -9 -9 +8 -7 -6s +7 +8
Ḡ   R̂ Ŝ N D R̂ R̂ Ŝ D M   P Ŝ

Sa - a - n - ta - a - a Lu - ci - a   San - ta Lu - ci - a
+10 +8 +8 +7 +7 +6 -6 -9 -9   -9 -7 -8 -9 +8
Ḡ   Ŝ Ŝ P P G m R̂ R̂   R̂   D   N R̂ Ŝ

San - ta Lu - ci - a
-9 +10 -9 -9 +8
R̂ Ḡ   R̂ R̂ Ŝ

Lesson 22: Santa Lucia

7.3 Jamaica Farewell

Once you have a good understanding on the rhythm with notes and gap, you can easily play the rhythmic tune - Jamaican Farewell on Harmonica. Idea behind providing the simple and cool music is to play them spontaneously from insight.

About the Song:

- Title: Jamaica Farewell
- Artist: Harry Belafonte
- Album: Calypso
- Language: English
- Released: 1956
- Genre: Mento / Jamaican Folk
- Songwriter: Irving Burgie

Tempo: Initially you can practice in slower speed, but gradually you can play Jamaican Farewell in little bit faster tempo (120 - 140).

About the Notation: Sheet Music is created on the same 4/4 beat in C Scale. Playing this type of song will help to understand the beats in much better way as there are lot of 1/8 notes and 1/8 gaps. In the staff note, we have used the lyrics of the Verse 1 and 2 out of total 8 verses.

About the Practice: It should be played at least 2-3 times while performing. But for practice, initially you should play 20 – 30 times.

Song Verses	Lyrics
Verse 1	Down the way Where the nights are gay And the sun shines daily on the mountaintop I took a trip on a sailing ship And when I reached Jamaica I made a stop
Verse 2	But I'm sad to say I'm on my way Won't be back for many a day My heart is down My head is turning around I had to leave a little girl in Kingston town
Verse 3	Down at the market you can hear Ladies cry out while on their heads they bear Ackee, rice, saltfish are nice And the rum is fine any time of year
Verse 4 (same as Verse 2)	But I'm sad to say I'm on my way Won't be back for many a day My heart is down My head is turning around I had to leave a little girl in Kingston town

Jamaica Farewell

Artist: Harry Belafonte | Album: Calypso | Released: 1956

- Simplified
- Harmonica Tabs
- Indian Notes
- by Riddhi Sanyal

Measures 1–2:
+7 P | +7 P | +7 P | +7 P | +7 P | -7 D | -8 N | +8 Ŝ | -8 N | -7 D

Measures 3–4:
+7 P | +7 P | -6 m | -6 m | +6 G | +6 G | -6 m | +7 P

Measures 5–6:
+7 P | +7 P | +7 P | +7 P | +7 P | -7 D | -8 N | +8 Ŝ | -8 N | -8 N | -7 D

Measures 7–8:
+7 P | +7 P | -6 m | -6 m | -6 m | +6 G | -5 R | +5 S | +6 G | +7 P

Measures 9–10:
+5 S | +5 S | +6 G | +6 G | -5 R | -5 R | -5 R | -6 m

Measures 11–12:
-4 N | -4 N | -5 R | +6 G | -5 R | +5 S | +5 S | -5 R | +6 G | +6 G

Measures 13–14:
+5 S | +5 S | +6 G | +6 G | +6 G | +6 G | -5 R | -5 R | -5 R | -6 m | -6 m | -6 m | -6 m

Measures 15–16:
+6 G | +6 G | +6 G | +6 G | -5 R | -5 R | +6 G | -5 R | +5 S

Lesson 23: Jamaica Farewell

7.4 Title Music – by Sri D. Madhusudan

This is one of the popular music composed by Guruji Sri. D. Madhusudan. This is played during the start of the musical concert and so it's named as Title Music. The quality of this tune will change anyone's mind into happy mood with full of positive vibes.

Composition Details:

- *Name: Title Music*
- *Composer: D. Madhusudan*
- *Year: 2013*
- *First performed by: Beniyasahakala in the year 2013-14*
- *Rhythm / Taal: 4/4 Beats, Keherwa taal.*
- *Tempo: 120 BPM*

Minor Notes: This tune is mostly on major. F# or M (Tibra Ma) is used at one location.

Why chosen for Harmonica: Title music can be played in both type of instruments such as Bowing or Strings. Particularly for Harmonica, we can play with little different than other instruments like – add harmony, add vibration to gain the long-lasting effect, create the rhythm and so on.

About the Notation: This tune has Bandish, Antara 1 and Antara 2. It's a straight forward tune and we may not return to Bandish after every Antara. So with a little swing, we can play like

Bandish → Antara 1 → Antara 2 → Antara 1 → End with higher octave of Antara 1

Having 10 – 12 holes, Harmonica has the advantage of Higher Octave till Pa or the Sa note. The max of Antara 1 reaches higher Pa which is on the limit of the Harmonica.

Title Music

Composer: D Madhusudan | Year: 2013

- Harmonica Notes
Maintained Originality
- by Riddhi Sanyal

End with higher octave of Antara 1

```
+8  -8 +8 -9 +8 -9  +10 -9 +10+11-10+10 -9 +8  -8 +8 -7  +7   +8
 Ŝ   N Ŝ  R̂  Ŝ  R̂   Ḡ  R̂  Ḡ  Ṗ  ḿ  Ḡ  R̂  Ŝ   N Ŝ  D   P    Ŝ
```

Lesson 24: Title Music – A Happy tune by D. Madhusudan

7.5 "O Sona Byang O Kola Byang" - Gems from Legend Salil Chowdhury

It's very difficult to produce a song for Kids. The reason it's difficult to tell the simple words in simple way. We have the Legend Salil Chowdhury as Indian music director and composer. He has produced lot of Bollywood songs, albums etc which forms the golden era of Indian music. I would like to choose one of his songs for our Harmonica practice.

The song details –

- ➢ *Song: O Sona Byang*
- ➢ *Singer: Antara Chowdhury*
- ➢ *Lyrics & music: Salil Chowdhury*
- ➢ *Year: 1979*
- ➢ *Pattern or Genre: Children's Music, Touch of Raga Yaman Kalyan*
- ➢ *Taal: 6/4 or 3/4 beats. Dadra Taal*
- ➢ *Tempo: Fast. Example: 160 – 240 bpm*

Song Meaning: The theme of the song is like this, a little girl is calling the *Byang* (frogs) to give the musical *talim* (initial lessons). She has given the *talim* to 2 categories of *Byang* (frogs) – Golden frogs and normal frogs. Our objective is to play the SARGAM given by **Salil Chowdhury** in the song. We will only those sections in our *Talim* (Initial lessons). The song lyrics are not separately given as we will only play the musical *SARGAM / Talim*. Though the language is on Bengali, but for music, language is not a barrier. You can find the popularity of this song in YouTube and you can find that it has millions and millions of views.

About the Notes & Beats: The Song is played on Dadra Taal in *Drut Laya* (faster tempo). Considering the Indian Musical Note, corresponding western notes are created in Staff Notes. You need to play this in little faster tempo like more than 160 bpm. Actual song was demonstrated in more than 240 bpm. This notation is created using the quarter note, half note and 3/4 th of whole note. For the simplicity and one to one comparison with Indian Note and Taal, this song was converted particularly in this fashion rather using 1/8 notes. Complete Indian *SARGAM* has been written on each of the western notes.

Key Learning's for Harmonica: So practicing this song will help you on –

- ➢ **Adopt to play in the same Taal / Metronome Tempo**
- ➢ **Learn 3/4 or 6/4 beats pattern.**
- ➢ **There is only one minor note, Tibra Ma = F# w.r.t. C.**

> **You will learn both Ma (F#) & ma (F) present in the same line / verse.**

O Sona Byang O Kola Byang
A Salil Chowdhury Song

- Simplified Notes
- Harmonica Tabs
- Indian Notes
by Riddhi Sanyal

♩ = 240 - Dadra Taal, Drut Laya

Pa	Pa	Pa	Pa	Ma	Pa	Dha	Pa	Re	Ga	ma	ma	ma	Ga	–	a
+7	+7	+7	+7	-6s	+7	-7	+7	-5	+6	-6	-6	-6	+6		+6
P	P	P	P	M	P	D	P	R	G	m	m	m	G		G

Ga	Ga	Re	Sa	Re	Re	Sa	Ni	Dha	Ni	Sa	Ni	Pa	–	a
+10	+10	-9	+8	-9	-9	+8	-8	-7	-8	+8	-8	+7		+7
Ġ	Ġ	Ř	Ŝ	Ř	Ř	Ŝ	N	D	N	Ŝ	N	P		P

Ba	ba	–	a	ba	ba	re	ba	–	h
Pa	Ga	Re	Ga	ma	Ga	Re	Sa		a
+7	+6	-5	+6	-6	+6	-5	+5		+5
P	G	R	G	m	G	R	S		S

Sa	Re	Ga	ma	Pa	Dha	Pa	Dha	Pa	ma	Ga
+5	-5	+6	-6	+7	-7	+7	-7	+7	-6	+6
S	R	G	m	P	D	P	D	P	m	G

Ga	ma	Pa	Dha	Ni	Sa	Re	Ni	Sa	Ni	Dha	Pa	ma	Ga
+6	-6	+7	-7	-8	+8	-9	-8	+8	-8	-7	+7	-6	+6
G	m	P	D	N	Ŝ	Ř	N	Ŝ	N	D	P	m	G

Ba	ba	–	a	ba	ba	re	ba	–	h
Pa	Ga	Re	Ga	ma	Ga	Re	Sa		a
+7	+6	-5	+6	-6	+6	-5	+5		+5
P	G	R	G	m	G	R	S		S

Lesson 25: O Sona Byang – a Salil Chowdhury Song

7.6 Hai Aapna Dil

This is one of the oldest Bollywood famous songs, where background music is played on Harmonica. All of the Interludes were originally played on Harmonica. The Interludes itself are very popular and most of the Harmonica players love to learn this. The Rhythm & Tune are so touchy that everyone loves this song.

About the Song:

- *Name: Hai Apna Dil To Aawara*
- *Singer: Hemant Kumar, Asha Bhosle, Mohd. Rafi*
- *Lyricist: Majrooh Sultanpuri*
- *Music Director: Sachin Dev Burman*
- *Film cast: Dev Anand, Waheeda Rehman, Bir Sakhuja, Sunder, Tun Tun*
- *Movie: Solva Saal*
- *Year: 1958*
- *Pattern or Genre: Indian Pop, Romantic*
- *Taal or Rhythm: 4/4 or Keherwa. It can also be played in 2/4 fashion.*
- *Tempo: Faster tempo like over 150 BPM is good for this song.*

About the notation & practice: Western notation has been created for this song. A few areas on the Interlude music of the song, the harmonics have been illustrated. Feel free to work on that when you play. With simple technique and capability like play the following together as applicable,

- **Play GC in place of C as both blows air and it's part of C Major chord**
- **Play EC in place of C as both blows air and it's part of C Major chord**
- **Play BD in place of B as both draws air and it's part of G Major chord**

So similarly you can improvise with this simple technique of 2 notes together at a time.

This song has lot of touchy notes or grace notes. A few are shown. You can add more if you feel.

This song can also be played with off-beat starting position. For simplicity, it's not shown in the notation as only Harmonica is given.

Lyrics: Only the first 2 verses (*Bandish* & First *Antara*) are given in the notation. Tune wise, it's almost identical for the remaining verses. After Bandish, every time **Interlude music 1** is repeated. Similarly in Antara, there is another music (**Interlude music 2**). Both of these Interlude music are on Harmonica in the original track. So this song is one of the most popular in Harmonica.

Song position	Lyrics
Bandish	Hai apanaa dil to aawaaraa, naa jaane kis pe aayegaa
Interlude Music 1	Original track has music in Harmonica
Antara 1	Haseenon ne bulaayaa, gale se bhee lagaayaa Bahut samjhayaa, yahee naa samajhaa + **Interlude Music 2** in Harmonica in original track Bahot bholaa hain bechaaraa, naa jaane kis pe aayegaa
Antara 2	Ajab hain diwaanaa, naa ghar naa thhikaanaa Jameen se begaanaa, Palak se judaa + **Interlude Music 2** in Harmonica in original track Ye ek tootaa huaa taaraa, naa jaane kis pe aayegaa

Hai Aapna Dil

Music Director: Sachin Dev Burman, Movie: Solva Saal (1958)

- Simplified Harmonica Notes by Riddhi Sanyal

♩ = 200

Bandish

Hai aa - p - na - a dil   To a - a wa - a - ra
+3 +4 +4   -5 -5 +6   +4 -5 +6 -5 +4 -4 -3
P S S   R R G   S R G R S N D

Na jaa - ne - e ki - s   Pe a - a - ye - e - ga
-4 +3   -3 -4 +4 +4   -5 +6 -5 +4 -5 +4 -4 +4
N P   D   N S S   R G S R S N S

Music Starts on Harmonica, one higher octave

[2.] e - ga
-4 +4
N S

+8 +8 -9 +10 -9 +10 +10 -9 +10   +8   -8 -7 +7 -7 +7 +7
+7 Ŝ Ř Ḡ   Ř   Ḡ   Ḡ   Ř Ḡ   Ŝ   N D P D P P
P

Fine / Music End

-8 +8 -9 +8 -9 -9 +8 -9 -10 +10 -9 +8 -9 +8 +8   +8 +10 -9 +8   +7   +8
N Ŝ Ř Ŝ Ř Ř Ŝ Ř   ᵐ   Ḡ   Ř Ŝ Ř Ŝ Ŝ   Ŝ Ḡ   Ř Ŝ   P   Ŝ

Antara 1

Ha - see - no ne bu - la - ya   ga - le se bhi la - gaa - ya
+4 +6 +6 +6   +6 -5s +6   +4 +6 +6 +6   +6 -5s +6
S G G G   G g   G   S G G G   G g   G

Ba - hut sam - jha - ya - a   yah - ee na sam -
+4 -6 -6   -6   -6 +6 -6   +7   +7 +7 -6
S   m   m   m   m   G m   P   P P m

[1.] **Music starts**   **Music ends**
jha - a
-6 +6 +7 -7 -8 +10 +10 +10 -8 -7 -8 -8 -8 -8   +7 +7 -7 -7 +7 -6 +6
m G P D N   +8 +8 +8 N -7 N N -7 -7   P P D D P   m G
              Ḡ   Ḡ   Ḡ   N   N N
              Ŝ   Ŝ   Ŝ   D   D D

[Sheet music excerpt with lyrics:]

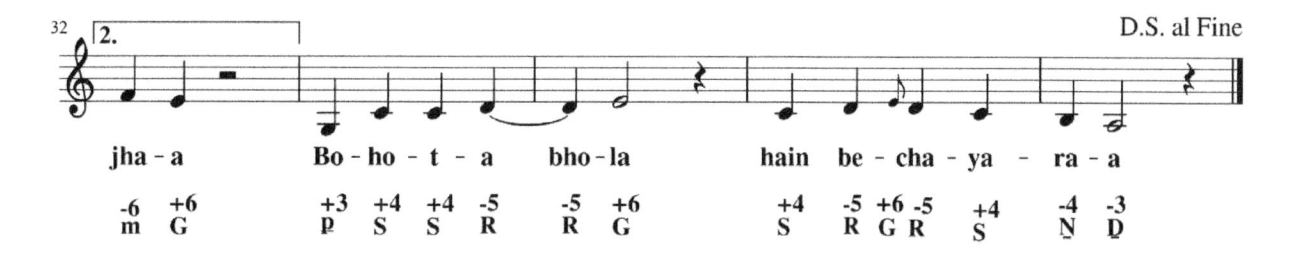

jha-a | Bo-ho-t-a bho-la | hain be-cha-ya-ra-a

-6 +6 | +3 +4 +4 -5 -5 +6 | +4 -5 +6 -5 +4 -4 -3
m G | P S S R R G | S R G R S N D

Lesson 26: Hai Aapna Dil

7.7 Minuet – Gems from Bach

Well this is a common tune for Piano in the Beginner – Intermediate level. I recommend this to play in Harmonica so that we will be more comfortable 3/4 beats. Rhythm & notes are the beauty of this notation.

About the Minuet –

- *Title: MINUET IN C*
- *Details: BWV Anh. 114*
- *Original By: Johann Sebastian Bach*
- *Tempo: Medium*
- *Beats / Taal: 3/4 Beats. Indian Taal is Dadra.*
- *Minor Notes: The only Minor Note used is Tibra Ma (M) or F# w.r.t. C.*

Notation: The original staff note was on the key of G. But for the Harmonica learners, I have changed the notation on the scale C. The notation has been simplified with the repeats so that it's more usable for the learners. The Harmonica blowing symbols are also attached with the notation so that it's more easier to relate from the Staff Notation.

Key Learning's for Harmonica:

- Unique 3/4 rhythm.
- Learn the quarter, eighth beats in the 3/4 beat notations
- Learn the Minor note F# or M (Tibra Ma)

Minuet

Details: BWV Anh. 114, Original By: Johann Sebastian Bach

- Simplified Staff Notes in C Major & Harmonica Tab Notes by Riddhi Sanyal

Measures 1–4:
+7 +5 −5 +6 −6 +7 +5 +5 −7 −6 +7 −7 −8 +8 +5 +5
P   S R G m P S S D m P D N Ŝ S S

Measures 5–6:
−6 +7 −6 +6 −5 +6 −6 +6 −5 +5
m P m G R G m G R S

Measures 7–10:
|1. −4 +5 −5 +6 +5 +6 −5 |2. −5 +6 −5 +5 −4 +5
   N S R G S G R   R G R S N S

Measures 11–12:
+10 +8 −9 +10 +8 −9 +7 −7 −8 +7
Ḡ   Ŝ R̂ Ḡ   Ŝ R̂ P D N P

Measures 13–14:
+8 −7 −8 +8 +7 −6s +6 −6s −5
Ŝ D N Ŝ P M   G M   R

Measures 15–18:
−5 +6 −6s +7 −7 −8 +8 −8 −7 −8 −5 −6s +7
R G M   P D N Ŝ N D N R M   P

Measures 19–22:
+7 +5 −4 +5 −7 +5 −4 +4 +7 −6 +6 −5 +5 −4 +5 −5
P S N S D S N S P m G R S N S R

Measures 23–26:
+3 −3 −4 +4 −5 +6 −6 +6 −5 +6 +7 +4 −4 +4
P D N S R G m G R G P S N S

Lesson 27: Minuet

7.8 Pran Chay Chokkhu Na Chay – A Rhythmic Song from Gurudev Sri Rabindranath Tagore

During this song practice, we will practice a nice rhythm. So we have chosen one of the Rhythmic songs from Gurudev Sri Rabindranath Tagore for our practice in Harmonica.

About the song:

- *Title: Pran Chay Chokkhu Na Chay*
- *Lyrics & Music Composition: Sri Rabindranath Tagore*
- *Category in Tagore Song: Prem (Love), sub-category: Prem-Boichitra*
- *Pattern, Genre or Raag: Bhairavi - Baul, Folk Based Song*
- *Year: 1914*
- *Location of the notation from Tagore: Swarabitan: 33 (Kabyageeti)*
- *Beating Pattern: It's in the Tritaal / Tin Taal which has 16 beats (4 – 4 – 4 – 4). That is represented as time signature 4 / 4.*
- *Tempo: Fast 180 – 220 bpm*

Chords Applicable to accompany: C, Dm, G, F, Am as suitable.

Song Structure: This song has *Bandish* & one *Antara*.

Minor / Sharp Notes:

- **Bb or n (Komal Ni)**
- **F# or M (Tibra Ma)**

About the Notation: This notation has been simplified in western and kept identical to Indian Notation. Hence the Tempo is more and each measure will have lesser notes. For example, mostly quarter notes and half notes are used in the notation. Lyrics are not separately given as it's the same in Notation.

Key Learning in Harmonica:

- **Minor scale (Phrygian mode) or Raga Bhairavi based tune to be learned in the easiest way in harmonica with changing the starting note. In this case, the start of the song is from Dha or A w.r.t. C Scale.**
- **Due to the change in scale, only Minor notes become Bb or n (Komal Ni) and F# or M (Tibra Ma). So that will help the Harmonica player to pick up the song easily.**

Pran Chay
A Rabindranath Tagore Song

- Harmonica Notes
Maintained Originality
- by Riddhi Sanyal

♩ = 220

Bandish

Pran — Chay
-7 / D — +7 / P

Chok -khu Na Chay -y -y -y Fine Mo -ri
+5 / S — -5 / R — +6 / G — +5 / S — -5 / R — +6 / G — -6 / m — +7 / P — +6 / G — -6 / m

E -ki To -or Dus -to -ro Loj -ja -a -a To Coda
-7 / D — +7 / P — -6 / m — +6 / G — -5 / R — +7 / P — +7 / P — -6 / m — +6 / G — -7 / D

Sun -do -ro E -se Phi -re Ja -ye -e -e To -be
-8 / N — -8 / N — -8 / N — -8 / N — -8 / N — -8 / N — -8 / N — -7 / D — -8 / N — +7 / P — -9 / R̂ — +8 / Ŝ — -8 / N

Kar La -gi Mi -it -tha E Soj -ja -a -a D.S. al Coda
-7 / D — -7s / n — -7 / D — +7 / P — -6s / M — +7 / P — +4 / S — -5 / R — +6 / G — -7 / D

Antara

Mu -khe Na -hi Nis -sore Bhas Do -he
+3 / P — -3 / D — -4 / N — +4 / S — -5 / R — -5 / R — -5 / R — +6 / G — +6 / G — +6 / G

An -to -re Ni -r -ba -ko Bon -hi
+3 / P — -3 / D — -4 / N — +4 / S — +4 / S — -5 / R — +6 / G — -6 / m — +6 / G

Lyrics	Notation	Sargam
Osh -the Ki Nis -thu -ro Ha -a -as To -bo	+7 +7 -6s +7 +7 -6s +6 -6 -7 +7 +7	P P M P P M G m D P P
Mor me Je Kron -do -no To nhi -i -i	+4 -5 +6 -5 +7 +7 -6 +6 +6 +6	S R G R P P m G G G
Mal -lyo Je Dan -shi -che Ha -a -ae -e Tor	+10 -10 +10 -9 +10 -9 -8 -9 +8 -8 -8	Ḡ ṁ Ḡ R̂ Ḡ R̂ N R̂ Ŝ N N
Shoj -ja Je Kon -to -ko Sho -oj -ja	-8 +8 -8 -7 -7s -7 +7 -6s +7	N Ŝ N D n D P M P
Mi -lo -no So -mud -ra Be -la -a -a -aa -e Chi -ro	+5 -5 +6 +5 -5 +6 +4 -5 -5 +6 +7 -6 +6	S R G S R G S R R G P m G
Bich -che -do Jor -jo -ro Moj -ja -a D.C. al Fine	+6 -6 +6 -5 +7 +7 -6 +6 -7	G m G R P P m G D

Lesson 28: Pran Chay Chokkhu Na Chay – A Rhythmic Tagore Song

7.9 Five Hundred Miles – Famous tune for Harmonica

Well, Harmonicas are very much suited for country side soothing music. Here is one of the best examples of that. We will learn to play Hundred Miles Song and I believe it's quite easy for you to pick up as if you can do that for one phrase, it's same for all. Just match the tune and slow rhythm and you are on.

About the Song:

- *Title: "500 Miles Away From Home"*
- *Singer: Single by Bobby Bare*
- *Album: 500 Miles Away From Home*
- *B-side "It All Depends on Linda"*
- *Released: September 1963*
- *Genre: Country Easy Listening*
- *Label: RCA Victor*
- *Songwriter(s): Hedy West*
- *Producer(s): Chet Atkins*
- *Bobby Bare singles chronology: "Detroit City" | (1963) "500 Miles Away From Home" | (1963) "Miller's Cave"*

Hindi: Indian composer Rajesh Roshan used the tune to compose song 'Jab Koyi Baat Bigad Jaaye' (English: "When Things Go Wrong") in 1990's movie Jurm".

Lyrics: Lyrics of first few phrases are given below. The tune of each phrase is identical.

Song position	Lyrics
Phrase 1	If you missed the train I'm on You will know that I am gone You can hear the whistle blow a hundred miles
	A hundred miles, a hundred miles A hundred miles, a hundred miles You can hear the whistle blow a hundred miles
Phrase 2	Lord, I'm one, Lord, I'm two Lord, I'm three, Lord, I'm four Lord, I'm five hundred miles away from home
	Away from home, away from home Away from home, away from home Lord, I'm five hundred miles away from home

Key Learning on Harmonica:

- **Simple slow rhythm on 4/4 beats**
- **This tune follows the Bhupali Raga with the notes - S R G P D Ŝ. So this will help us to practice the songs related to Bhupali Raga.**

Five Hundred Miles

Singer: Single by Bobby Bare | Songwriter(s): Hedy West | Album: 500 Miles Away From Home

- Simplified Staff Notes & Harmonica Tab Notes by Riddhi Sanyal

If you miss the train I'm on

+5	+5	+6	+6	-5	+5	+6
S	S	G	G	R	S	G

If you know that I am gone

-5	+5	-5	+6	-5	+5	-3
R	S	R	G	R	S	D

You can hear the wis - tle blo - w a

-3	+5	-5	+6	-5	+5	-3	+3	+3
D	S	R	G	R	S	D	P	P

Hun - dred mile - s

-3	+5	-5	-5
D	S	R	R

Hun - dred miles a hun - dred miles A

+5	+5	+6	+6	-5	+5	+6	+6
S	S	G	G	R	S	G	G

Hun - dred miles A Hun - dred miles

-5	+5	-5	+6	-5	+5	-3
R	S	R	G	R	S	D

You can hear the wis - tle blo - w a

-3	+5	-5	+6	-5	+5	-3	+3	+3
D	S	R	G	R	S	D	P	P

Hun - dred mile - s

-3	+5	+5	+5
D	S	S	S

Lesson 29: Five Hundred Miles

7.10   Music for Wind – Created by Guruji Sri D. Madhusudan

This is one the finest music by Guruji Sri. D. Madhusudan to perform on Harmonica & other wind instruments. We have combined 3 ways of notations together for this similar to other songs.

About the Tune:

- *Name: Music for Wind*
- *Composed By: D. Madhusudan*
- *Year of Publication: 2020*
- *Taal or Rhythm: Waltz rhythm, 3/4, Dadra Taal*
- *Tempo: Slow*
- *First performed by: Beniyasahakala, the musical band.*

More on the Tune: We remember when Guruji gifted this music to us for practice. That was during Covid situation and everyone was mentally down. This tune just simply purifies your mind and soul with the deep feeling. Always play with Vibration as much as you can to get the feel. Some of the song location, we have added the Vibration symbol. Feel free to improvise. Also few areas you can apply bending technique to smoothly change the notes.

This tune can be best played in the following wind instruments –

- **Harmonica**
- **Saxophone**
- **Flute**
- **Melodica**

Key learning's on Harmonica:

- **Vibration or Note bending are the main factors to create the feel.**

Music For Wind - Waltz Rhythm

Composed By: Sri D. Madhusudan, Year of Publication: 2020

- Simplified Staff Notes in C Major & Harmonica Tab Notes by Riddhi Sanyal

♩ = 80

Bandish - Verse 1   *fff*

+6 -5 +5 +6   +6 -5 +5 -6
G   R   S   G   G   R   S   m

Play with Vibration & Bending style   Fine / To Coda

-6 +6 -5 +7 -7 +6 +6
m   G   R   P   D   G   G

Antara - Verse 2

-7 -8 +8   +7 -7 -8
D   N   Ŝ   P   D   N

D.S. al Coda

-6 +7 -7 +7 -6 +6 +6
m   P   D   P   m   G   G

+5 +5 +5 -5 -4   +5 +5 +5 -5 -3
S   S   S   R   Ṉ   S   S   S   R   Ḏ

-4 -4 -4 -5 -6   +7 -6 +6
N   N   N   R   m   P   m   G

-7 -7 +8 -8 -7   -6 -6 -6 -5 +6
D   D   Ŝ   N   D   m   m   m   R   G

D.S. al Coda

-5 -5 -6 -8   +7 -6 +6
R   R   m   N   P   m   G

Antara - Verse 3

+6   +5   -4 -3   -3
G   S   N D   D

-5   -4   -3 +3   +3
R   N   D P   P

+5   +6   -6   -7   -7
S   G   m   D   D

D.S. al Fine

+7   -6   +6   +6
P   m   G   G

Lesson 30: Music for Wind – Waltz rhythm

7.11 Further Learning

There are some more songs for you to explore on your own. We have listed the intermediate level songs.

- **Bachelor Boys**

This is the famous song by "**Cliff Richard**". To Start this song, you can play from

Indian Notes:

"Ŝ Ŝ Ŝ | G m P | D P m | D – –"

"N N N | D P m | P – –"

Western Notes:

"Ĉ Ĉ Ĉ | E F G | A G F | A – –"

"B B B | A G F | G – –"

What is the Rhythm? Yes, you are right. It's on 3/4 beats.

- **Galyat sankali sonya chi, Hi pori kona chi - A famous Goan Folk Song**

This is a Folk song from Goa / Konkani region of India. You can start the first line like

Indian Notes:

"G G G | G G G | R G R | S – – | S R G | m – G | – R – |".

Western Notes:

"E E E | E E E | D E D | C – – | C D E | F – E | – D – |".

No minor needed. This is a nice folk rhythm. Play and enjoy.

- **Titanic Song**

This is about the Titanic theme song by **Celine Dion**. You can start with

Indian Notes:

"S – S S S | N̲ S – S | N̲ S – R | G – R –"

Western Notes:

"C – C C C | B̲ C – C | B̲ C – D | E – D –"

It's on simple 4/4 beats. But the notes sometime starts like off-beat position that you have to be careful about.

> **Phoolon Ke Rang Se**

You have already played Waltz rhythm 3/4 during the intermediate level songs. Once you have played Minuet there, you should be comfortable on the rhythm. Well this song "Phoolon Ke Rang Se", by Kishore Kumar from the Movie "Prem Pujari" composed by S. D. Burman, is one of the melodist song that can be played on Harmonica. You can start this song like

Indian Notes:

"G G :G | g G – | G G :G | g G – | ⍰ D N | S R G | mG R – | …"

Western Notes:

"E E :E | D# E – | E E :E | D# E – | G A B| C D E | FE D – | …"

You will find that you need to play couple of minor notes in this song

> g ~ Eb / D#
> M ~ F# / Gb

This song will look easier than Minuet. Discover and play yourself.

> **Gazab Ka Hai Din**

Please refer to the original song "Gazab Ka Hai Din", Album : Qayamat Se Qayamat Tak (1988), Singer : Alka Yagnik, Udit Narayan, Musician : Anand, Milind and Lyricist : Majrooh Sultanpuri. That song has excellent feel and soft rocking rhythm which turns out identical to play on Harmonica.

You have the notes and gaps here together similar to Five Hundred miles which you have already played in this section. Here you have more gaps. You can start like this and find your own notes –

Indian Notes:

"GPP mm – – | GGR SR – – | GP PDm – – | GGR SR – – |"

Western Notes:

"EGG FF – – | EED CD – – | EG GAF – – | EED CD – – |"

You can see that there are 2 / 3 notes together to play and there are long gaps. That's the unique pattern you have to follow here.

8.0 Advance Level Songs / Tunes for Harmonica

Slowly we have completed the beginners and intermediate and arrive at some more interesting Tune or Rhythms. To start with the tunes or songs from the Advance Level, we expect the learner,

- To play confidently and consistently in same tempo.
- Can play 3/4 and 4/4 beats.
- Can play single note as well as multiple notes simultaneously.
- Can play any minor notes.
- Can play in Note Bending style
- Can play with Vibration
- Can read the notation in any one form – Sheet Music, Harmonica Tabs or Indian Notes as described in Chapter 2.

Learning Period for the Advance Lessons:

- This section will take approximately 30 – 50 days of your days of practice assuming you can pick up one song within 3 - 5 days.
- You should add on the further learning section of 5 more songs within 10 – 15 days.
- Overall, if you sincerely practice daily, you can target to play all of the tunes and songs within 3 - 4 months.

Here is the summary for you on the Advance level songs or tunes and why they are chosen, for instance the learning's from these tunes.

SL	Name	Genre	Rhythm	Taal	Tempo	Level	Learning On Harmonica
1	The Lion King Song	Pop, soft rock	4/4	Keherwa	Medium. Ex: 120 BPM	Intermediate to Advance	• Create the feel of the song with Vibration as needed • Note bending technique in a few areas will give a nice feel.
2	March Music	Marching	4/4	Keherwa	Slow	Advance	• A totally different rhythm with Triplets • Rhythm swing from Western to Indian Style (in 4/4)
3	Chala Jata Hoon	Indian Pop, Romantic	4/4	Keherwa	Fast	Intermediate to Advance	• Rhythm is tricky to follow as it's depicting running car in Himalayas with lot of turns. • Play with Vibration to get the feel. • Harmonica can give the essence of yodeling sound by Kishore.
4	Tomay Hrid Majhare Rakhbo	Indian Folk Song, Baul, Loke Geeti, Kirtan	3/4	Dadra	Fast	Advance	• Fast rhythm on 3/4 beats • Idea on Indian Folk Music, Baul song.
5	Waltz 12	Soft Rock, Harmony	3/4	Dadra	Medium to Fast	Advance	• All 12 notes will be practiced by this. • Scale changing to consider F or ma as Sa during the middle of the song. • Vibration to generate feel
6	Surero Ei Jhor Jhor Jhorna	World Music, Harmonic Rhythm	4/4	Keherwa	Fast	Advance	• Interlude music has full of Harmonic Rhythm • Generate strokes in Harmonica with short breath control. That will ease the rhythm creation in Harmonica
7	Yeh Dosti Hum Nahi Todenge	Indian Pop, Friendship	4/4	Keherwa	Fast	Advance	• Playing rhythmic song and create rhythm in Harmonica • Simulating Harmonica chords • Playing note bending & vibration as needed
8	Ajib Dastan Hai Yeh	Country, Jazz Rhythm	4/4	Keherwa	Medium	Advance	• Playing the Jazz Rhythm • Vibration will help to generate the feel. • Interlude will help us to play end to end.
9	Salute to Covid Warriors	Dorian Melody	3/4 Waltz	Dadra	Slow	Advance	• Dorian Mode (Kafi Thaat) music is given for practice in the original scale, Ex C scale. That will give control in Eb or g (komal ga) and Bb or n (Komal ni). • Off Beat in the *Antara* will help you judge the beat.
10	Mere Sapno Ki Rani Kab Aayegi Tu	Indian Pop, Romantic, Bhairavi, Phrygian mode or Minor Scale	4/4	Keherwa	Medium to Fast	Advance	• Phrygian mode music practice. For Harmonica, it's simplified by starting from E in the C scaled Harmonica. • Concept of Bhairavi will be coming into players mind. • Playing train sound like rhythm. • More understanding on Off-Beat. • Interlude is on E major chord which has minor notes w.r.t. C scale. More idea on the scales with Major & Minor chords.

Table 9: Advanced Level Tunes & summary on the learning

8.1 The Lion King Song

Once you play till this, you should already gain the understanding of different beats with Gaps like 1/2, 1/4, 1/8 beats. This is one of the best romantic songs. "Can You Feel the Love Tonight", the Song title tells the same too.

About the Song:

- Song Name: Can You Feel the Love Tonight
- Artist: Elton John
- Movie: The Lion King
- Released: 1994
- Genre: Pop, soft rock
- Label: Walt Disney Mercury
- Composer(s): Elton John
- Lyricist(s): Tim Rice
- Producer(s): Chris Thomas
- Rhythm / Taal: 4/4. Indian Taal is Keherwa.
- Tempo: Medium

External Links for original Song, Lyrics / Credits:

- View & Listen to Original Song: https://www.youtube.com/watch?v=KjgWWjkNbhU
- View Lyrics: https://genius.com/Walt-disney-records-can-you-feel-the-love-tonight-lyrics

About the Notation & Practice:

We have created the notation of this song in higher octave in sheet music as this is touching lot of lower notes (Example: lower E, lower D). For Harmonica, it does not matter as it supports entire Lower Octave. For 10 holes Harmonica, please follow the notation as given. If your Harmonica is 12 hole, then you can play at higher octave.

As this is of Soft-Rock type, performers are free to start or end the lines in off-beat mode. As long as the 4/4 beating patterns are followed, we should be good. The notation of the interlude music piece is also created. The same music piece is played at the start and at the middle of the song before Para 3.

We have 4 verses to this song. Among them, tune of Para 3 has is identical to Para 1 with different lyrics. Whereas Para 4 is just a repeat of Para 2. While making the notation, we have only created the notation for Music + Para 1 + Para 2. While playing the complete song in Harmonica, you need to repeat the entire notation and that will give you the flavour of entire song.

About the Original Scale: The original scale of the song is Bb. But since all of the notations of this book are created in the scale C, same has been followed here also.

How to play with Rhythm: First practice the notation thoroughly. To build the notes of full song, you can create the notation of Para 3 in your notepad copying the Para 1. Para 4 will be identical with Para 2.

Key Learning's:

- **Create the feel of the song with Vibration as needed.**
- **Note bending technique in a few areas will give a nice feel.**
- **Learn the beats with Gaps on 1/2, 1/4, 1/8 beats.**

Can You Feel the Love Tonight

Artist: Elton John | Movie: The Lion King | Released: 1994

- Simplified Notes Harmonica Tabs, Indian Notes by Riddhi Sanyal

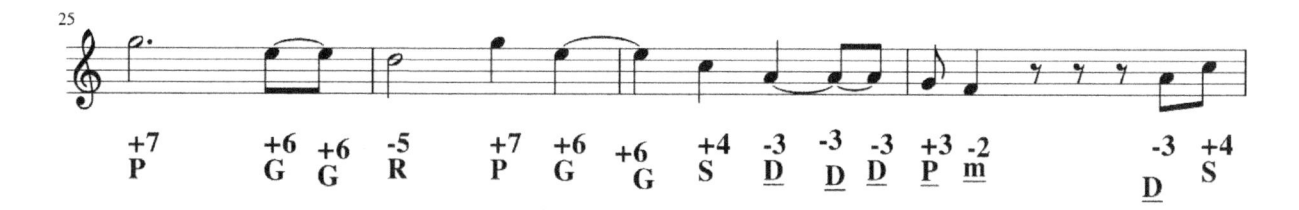

Music Starts

+6 +6 -5 +7 -6 -6 -6 +6 +4 +3
G   G   R   P   m   m   m   G   S   P

Music ends

-3 +3 +4 +3 +2 -1 +2 +3 -3
D   P S P G R   G   P   D

Song Verse 1 starts. Ex: There's a calm ...

-3 -4 +4 -5 +4 +4 +3   -3 -4 +4 -5 +4   +4
D N S R S S P   D N S R S   S

-3 -4 +4 -5 +4 +4 +3 +6   -6 +6 -5 +6 +4 -5
D N S R S S P G   m G R G S R

-3 -4 +4 -5 +4 +4 +3   -3 -4 +4 -5 +4 +4
D N S R S S P   D N S R S S

-3 -4 +4 +3 +3 +7 +6 +4 -3 -6 +6 -5 +6 -5 -5 +3
D N S P P P G S D m G R G R R P

Main Line - Can you feel the love ...

+7 +6 +6 -5 +7 +6 +6 +4 -3 -3 -3 +3 -2   -3 +4
P   G G R   P G G   S D D D P m   D S

Lesson 31: Can You Feel the Love Tonight – The Lion King Song

8.2 March Music – Composed by Sri D. Madhusudan

March music, the music for marching was first composed by Guruji Sri. D. Madhusudan on the year of 2013-14. When we played this first time, we have realized the power of this tune. Guruji has given this for our practice initially, but slowly it became popular. Then we really performed this by marching in one of the Independence Day program.

About this Composition:

- *Name: March Music*
- *Composed By: D. Madhusudan*
- *First Performed by Academy of Beniyasahakala*
- *Year of Composition: 2014*
- *Rhythm: Try to play with any Marching Rhythm from Piano or Metronome or any rhythm app.*
- *Tempo: You can play at 100 BPM or more.*
- *Minor Notes: Minor ni, symbol n (Bb w.r.t C) and Tibra Ma (F# w.r.t. C) in couple of places only.*
- *Length: just over 2 mins.*

Grand Orchestra performance:

During 2022 Annual function at Kolkata, this March Music tune was performed by around 40 musicians – Wind Instruments - Flute, String Instruments – Mandolin, Guitar, Violin, Cello, multiple percussions – Octapad (western) and Tabla, etc. It was really a grand orchestra and a wonderful harmony to play this all together. Kids under 10 years of age to Adults over 50 years age played this together along with Guruji who directed the rhythm from Guitar.

March Music

Composed By: Sri D. Madhusudan, Year of Publication: 2014

- Simplified Staff Notes in C Major & Harmonica Tab Notes by Riddhi Sanyal

Lesson 32: March Music by D. Madhusudan – March rhythm

8.3 Chala Jata Hoon

Chala Jata Hoon is one of the best romantic songs by Kishore Kumar. Legendary music director, R D Burman has depicting the momentum of driving a car in Himalayan Mountains. Kishore Kumar ji has created a different mood by changing his voice at the higher notes and similarly we can also play the harmonica with a vibrating flavour for those notes.

About the Song:

- *Name: Chala Jata Hoon*
- *Album / Movie: Mere Jeevan Saathi*
- *Singer: Kishore Kumar*
- *Composer: R D Burman*
- *Lyricist: Majrooh Sultanpuri*
- *Year: 1972*
- *Publisher: Saregama*
- *Features: Rajesh Khanna, Tanuja*
- *Rhythm / Taal: 4/4 or Keherwa Taal.*

Beating Pattern: The beating pattern of this song can be is "DaRa – DaRa – DaDa". Representing in another way, from 1 to 8 with beats as numbers, gaps with "–", it will look like: 12 – 45 – 78. Representing in Tabla *bol*: "Dha Dhin – Na Dhin – Te Te". You will find the similar beating pattern in the famous Bollywood song "Musafir Hoon Yaron" Song by Kishore Kumar.

Minor Notes: Bb (Komal Ni) – symbol n) at one location.

Why chosen for Harmonica: The notes and rhythms are so catchy that you will love to sing this or play this in light mood. Soft instruments like Harmonica can give you the feeling of original mood & rhythm. We will learn a lot after learning this like –

- **Learn this particular 4/4 rhythm**
- **Learn to vibrate the notes which sustains**
- **Play and pause to generate the rhythm of a running car**

About the Notes & Practice: There are 3 Antara in the song along with the Bandish / Sthayi. Only first Antara has been given in the notation whereas each Antara has identical tune. Tune of the last 2 lines of Bandish (section marked as $ in Notation) is identical to every Antara in terms of they are ending with same tune. Example: the tune of the phrase "Milan ki masti, bhari aankho me…" matches with the phrase "Mere jivan me, ye shaam aai hai …". So in the lyrics table, that is separately shown to memorize easily.

The sections, which you can vibrate or slight bend, have been marked with Vibration in the notation. You can experiment the vibration on any measure which is sustained.

Lyrics:

Phrases	Lyrics
Bandish	Chalaa jaataa hun, kisi ki dhun me
	Dhadakate dil ke, taraane liye
Bandish last 2 lines (Denoted as $ in Notation) – (common tune after every Antara)	Milan ki masti, bhari aankho me
	Hazaaro sapane, suhaane liye
Antara 1	Ye masti ke, nazaare hai, to aise me
	Sambhalanaa kaisaa meri qasam
	Tu laharaati, dagariyaa ho, to phir kyun naa
	Chalun mai bahakaa bahakaa re
Antara 1 last 2 lines - Tune same with Bandish section $	Mere jivan me, ye shaam aai hai
	Muhabbat vaale, zamaane liye,
Antara 2	Vo aalam bhi, ajab hogaa, vo jab mere
	Karib aaegi meri qasam
	Kabhi baiyyaa chhudaa legi, kabhi hansake
	Gale se lag jaaegi haay
Antara 2 last 2 lines - Tune same with Bandish section $	Meri baaho me, machal jaaegi
	Vo sachche jhuthe bahaane liye
Antara 3	Bahaaro me, nazaaro me, nazar daalun
	To aisaa laage meri qasam
	Vo naino me, bhare kaajal, ghughat khole
	Khadi hai mere aage re
Antara 3 last 2 lines - Tune same with Bandish section $	Sharam se bojhal jhuki palako me
	Javaan raato ke fasaane liye

Chala Jata Hoon

Singer: Kishore Kumar, Composed By: R D Burman,
Movie: Mere Jeevan Saathi (1972)

- Simplified Staff Notes in C Major & Harmonica Tab Notes by Riddhi Sanyal

♩ = 180 **Bandish**

Cha-la jaa-ta hoon   Ki-si ki dhun me
+6 +6 +6 +7   +7   +6 +6 +5 -6   -6
G G   G   P   P   G G   S   m   m
                                         To Coda Fine

Dhadak-te dil ke   Taa-ra-ne li-ye — e
+6 +6 +6 +7   +7   +6 +5 -5 -4 +5   +5
G G   G   P   P   G S   R   N̲ S   S

Last 2 lines of Bandish.
All Antara ends with this same tune

Mi-lan ki mas-ti   Bha-ri aan-kho me
Me-re   ji-van — me   Ye shaam aa — i hai
+8 +8   -8 -7   -7   -8 -8   -7 +7   +7
Ŝ Ŝ   N   D   D   N N   D   P   P
                                         D.S. al Coda

Haa-za-ro swap ne   Su-ha-ne li-ye-e e
Mu-ha-bhat vaa le   Za-ma-ne li-ye-e e
+8 +8 -8 -7   -7   -8 -8 -7 +7   +7 -6 +6
Ŝ Ŝ   N   D   D   N N   D   P   P m G

Antara 1

Ye mas-ti ke — e   Na-za-re ha-i — i
+7 +7 +7 +7 +10 +10   +7 +7 +7 +7 -10 +10
P P   P   P   Ḡ   Ḡ   P P   P   P   ṁ   Ḡ

Lesson 33: Chala Jata Hoon – Sheet Music with Harmonica Notes

8.4 Indian Folk Music – Tomay Hrid Majhare Rakhbo

This is one of the popular Folk song in Bengali. This tune is a very much popular in entire eastern India. Idea is to familiarize with Indian Folk Song and the typical rhythm.

About the Song:

- Song: Tomay Hrid Majhare Rakhbo (তোমায় হৃদ মাঝারে রাখবো)
- Lyrics: Dwij Bhushan
- Music: Vaishnav Kirtan
- Category: Indian Folk Song, Baul, Loke Geeti, Kirtan
- Taal: Fast Dadra or 3/4 rhythm. Best feeling will get when you play with the percussion Sri Khol.
- Tempo: Fast

This song has been performed by many artists: Lopamudra Mitra, Bolepur Bluez, Laxman Das, Gautam Das baul, Akriti Kakar, Sahaj Ma, Aditi munshi, Kalika Prasad Bhattacharya from Dohar Band And Many Others in their own way. This Baul Song Is Sung By Anusheh Anadil From Coke studio Bangla.

Why chosen for Harmonica: Well it's time to learn the fast rhythm with folk. This song has little touch of Raga Bhupali too. That will have ease of playing in Harmonica compared to other folks.

Lyrics:

Section	Lyrics
Bandish	Tomay hrid majhare rakhibo chere debo na Ore chere dile sonar Gour ar pabo na Khepa chere dile sonar Gour ar pabo na
Antara 1	Bhubono mohono gora, Gopi jonar mono hora Ore Radhar preme matowara Chand gour amar, Radhar preme matowara Dhulay jay bhai gora-gori Jete chaile jete debo na
Antara 2	Jabo brojer kule kule Amra makhbo paaye ranga dhuli Ore noyonete noyon diye rakhbo tare chole gele jete debo na na na

About the Notation: Baul / Folk notes are really difficult to create as there are 1/8 beats in 3/4 Taal. To give an idea on Indian Folk music, this song has been chosen for Harmonica. We will learn the beating pattern in Indian folk song and try to play the lyrics with the rhythm. Baul / folk songs has open environment to play as you may wait for one cycle of rhythm or repeat one verse for more than once. As long as you are enjoying the rhythm, tune, lyrics, you are welcome to play for multiple times. Each Antara has similar in tune. Only the first one has been created in Notes.

Learning's on Harmonica:

- **Fast rhythm on 3/4 beats**
- **Idea on Indian Folk Music, Baul song.**

Tomay Hrid Majhare Rakhbo Chere Debo Na

Lyricist: Dwij Bhushan | Music: Vaishnav Kirtan

- Harmonica Notes
Maintained Originality
- by Riddhi Sanyal

♩ = 140 **Bandish**   Fine   To Coda

To - may hrid ma - jha - re ra - kh - bo che - re de - bo na

| +5 | -5 | +6 | +6 | +6 | -5 | +6 | -7 | +7 | +6 | -5 | +6 | -5 | +5 |
| S | R | G | G | G | R | G | D | P | G | R | G | R | S |

Ore - e che - re di - le so - nar Go - ur ar pa - bo - o na - a

Khe-pa

| +7 | -7 | +8 | +8 | +8 | +8 | +8 | +8 | +8 | -8 | -7 | -8 | +8 | -8 | -7 | +7 |
| P | D | Ŝ | Ŝ | Ŝ | Ŝ | Ŝ | Ŝ | Ŝ | N | D | N | Ŝ | N | D | P |

D.S. al Coda

bo - o na na - a na che - re de - bo na

| +8 | -8 | -7 | +7 | -7 | +7 | +6 | -5 | +6 | -5 | +4 |
| Ŝ | N | D | P | D | P | G | R | G | R | S |

Bhu-ba-no mo-ha-n-o Go-ra - a   a   Go-pi jo-ner

									-6	+6	-5				
									m	G	R				
+5	+5	+5	-5	-5	+6	-6	-5	+6		+6		-5	-5	-5	-5
S	S	S	R	R	G	m	R	G		G		R	R	R	R

mo - no ho - ra - a

				-5		+4
				R		S
-5	+6	-6	+6			
R	G	m	G			

Bhu-ba-no mo-ha-no Go-ra - a   a

								-9	+10	
								Ř	G	-9	+8
+6	+6	+7	-7	-7	+8	-8	+8	+8			
G	G	P	D	D	Ŝ	N	Ŝ	Ŝ		Ř	Ŝ

Go - pi jo - ner mo - no ho - ra

| -8 | -8 | -8 | -8 | -7 | +8 | -8 | -7 | +7 |
| N | N | N | N | D | Ŝ | N | D | P |

Page | 107 | Advance Level Songs / Tunes for Harmonica | **Mouth Organ For Everyone**

Copyright © 2022 India. All Rights Reserved

RIDDHI SANYAL

Lesson 34: Indian Folk Song - Tomay Hrid Majhare Rakhbo

8.5   Waltz 12 By D. Madhusudan – 12 Notes Practice

During this lesson, we will learn one of the best compositions from Guruji Sri D. Madhusudan. This is on the Waltz Rhythm which can be represented as 3/4 or in 6 beats Dadra Taal. The best part of the composition is it contains all 12 notes which are very rare to be observed in a single composition. Guruji told while creating of the composition, he has done the scale change smoothly from C to F and in such a wonderful way that you will not realize until you listen to the full song. Again the beauty is to transition back from F to C scale.

About this Composition:

- *Name: Waltz 12*
- *Composed By: D. Madhusudan*
- *First Performed by Academy of Beniyasahakala*

- Year of Composition: 2021
- Rhythm: Try to play with Waltz Rhythm from Piano or 3/4 Beats in Metronome.
- Tempo: You can play at 180 BPM or more.
- Minor Notes: All Minor and major notes.
- Taal / Rhythm: Dadra or Waltz. 3/4 beats.
- Length: 2 - 3 mins.

About the Notes & Practice: This Tune has 4 verses and can be played in a straight forward manner. The end of the tune touches a satire mood. Guruji tells that our life is like a musical stream which sometime has happy moods and sometimes the sad part. This music itself represents both the moods of our life. No need to repeat the *Bandish* Verse at the end from the composer. If you want to bring the happy mood again, you can play the *Bandish* Verse at the end.

Some of the phrases are marked with Vibration. Please play with the Vibration & slight bending of the notes to yield that bend effect.

Learning's on Harmonica:

- **All 12 notes will be practiced by this.**
- **During the middle of the song, there is a Scale change to F or ma. That will help you to realize how the notation changes when we shift to F or ma.**
- **Play with vibration to generate feeling.**

Waltz 12 - Best for 12 Notes Practice

- Simplified Staff Notes in C Major & Harmonica Tab Notes by Riddhi Sanyal

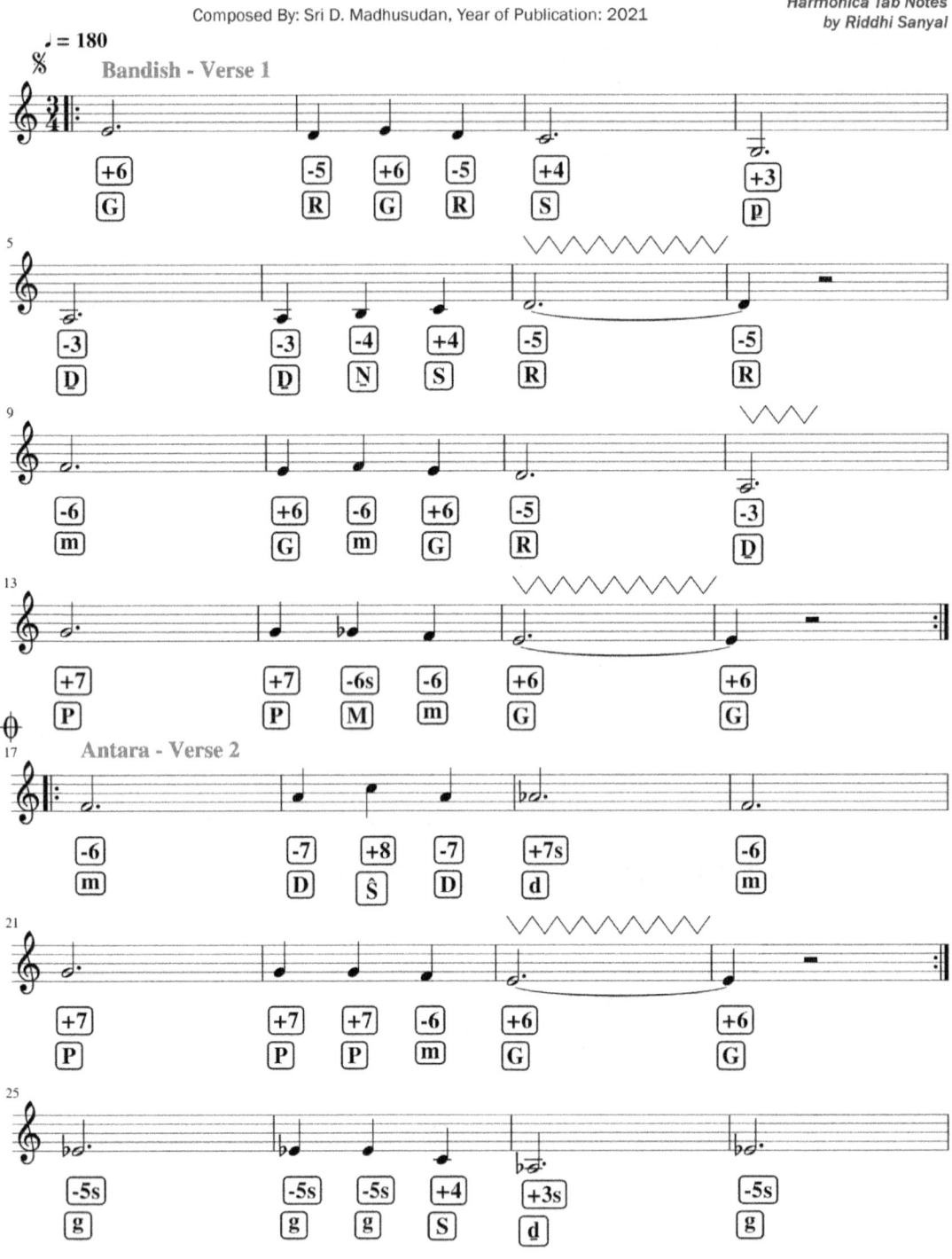

Composed By: Sri D. Madhusudan, Year of Publication: 2021

♩ = 180

Bandish - Verse 1

+6	-5	+6	-5	+4	+3
G	R	G	R	S	P

-3	-3	-4	+4	-5	-5
D	D	N	S	R	R

-6	+6	-6	+6	-5	-3
m	G	m	G	R	D

+7	+7	-6s	-6	+6	+6
P	P	M	m	G	G

Antara - Verse 2

-6	-7	+8	-7	+7s	-6
m	D	Ŝ	D	d	m

+7	+7	+7	-6	+6	+6
P	P	P	m	G	G

-5s	-5s	-5s	+4	+3s	-5s
g	g	g	S	d	g

Antara - Verse 3

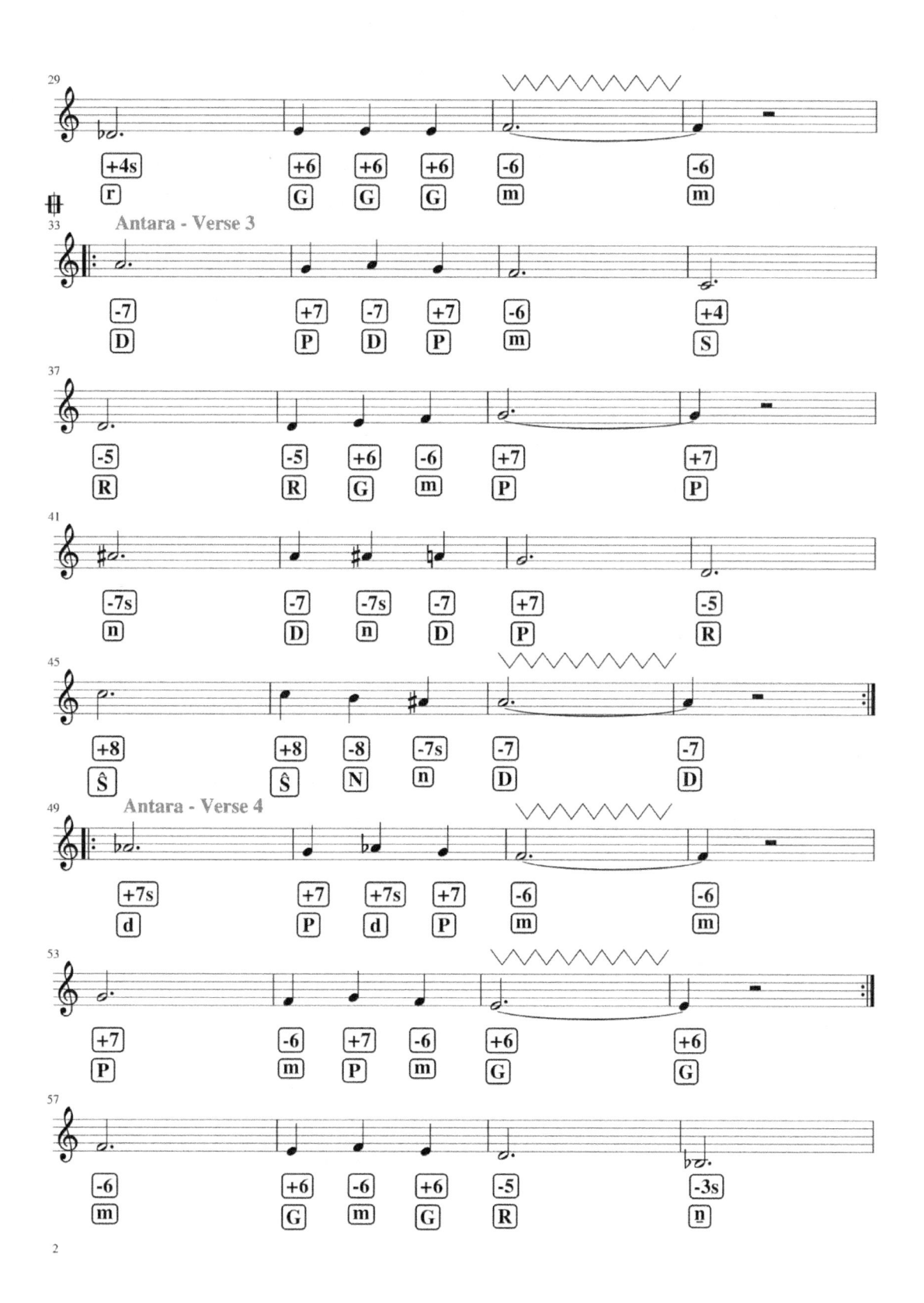

| +4s | +6 | +6 | +6 | -6 | -6 |
| r | G | G | G | m | m |

| -7 | +7 | -7 | +7 | -6 | +4 |
| D | P | D | P | m | S |

| -5 | -5 | +6 | -6 | +7 | +7 |
| R | R | G | m | P | P |

| -7s | -7 | -7s | -7 | +7 | -5 |
| n | D | n | D | P | R |

| +8 | +8 | -8 | -7s | -7 | -7 |
| Ŝ | Ŝ | N | n | D | D |

Antara - Verse 4

| +7s | +7 | +7s | +7 | -6 | -6 |
| d | P | d | P | m | m |

| +7 | -6 | +7 | -6 | +6 | +6 |
| P | m | P | m | G | G |

| -6 | +6 | -6 | +6 | -5 | -3s |
| m | G | m | G | R | n |

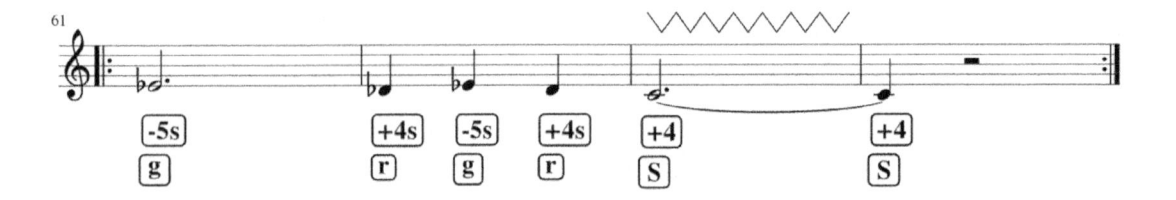

Lesson 35: Waltz 12 by D. Madhusudan – Waltz rhythm

8.6 Surero Ei Jhor Jhor Jhorna – Learn Rhythm from Salil Chowdhury's song

This was one of the beauties in Harmonics by legendary music director Salil Chowdhury. The song, the interlude music, lyrics, everything have full of harmony, which takes us into a different world. Hence this song is best suites on the Harmonica compared to other instruments.

About the song:

- *Song: Surer Ei Jharjhar Jharna*
- *Artist: Sabita Chowdhury*
- *Album: "Mon-Mayuri Chharalo Pekham" - Sabita Chowdhury*
- *Song Credits & Publisher: Saregama India Ltd*
- *Taal: 4/4 Rhythm. Keherwa taal.*

Tempo: Very fast rhythm like 200 bpm. Orignal song is even more than that. In this speed, 200 bpm, most of the notation beat length are 1/8, 1/4 and 1/2.

Music: The Intro, Interlude music is also created here in the staff notes. That will help us to learn and create fast rhythm on Harmonica. This music of the song will help us to play in chord like fashion. The original has been sung by additional vocal artists only to create harmonics. Here while playing the song; if multiple instrument players are there, you can play in different octaves to generate the harmonics.

Learning's on Harmonica:

- **Interlude music has full of Harmonic Rhythm.**

- **For generating the Harmonic sound, 2 notes are given to play simultaneously. That is followed in few areas in the notation. The Harmonic flavour will help you to enjoy the rhythm as well as the concept of chords played during the Harmonics.**
- **Generate strokes in Harmonica with short breath control. That will ease the rhythm creation in Harmonica.**

Only the first Antara has been given in the lyrics and notation. Antara 2 has same sound.

Phrases	Lyrics
Bandish	Surera o ei jharo jharo jharana,
	Jharana hai mari hai mari hai re
	Jharana jhare re
	Durero ei gun gun gunjan
	Dujanai jai chole jai chole jai re
	Rahena ghare re (Sounds same as first 3 lines)
	Jharana jhare re, rahena ghare re
	Jharana jhare re, rahena ghare re (Lines Repeated)
Antara 1	Meghe meghe meghabalika abirao dhale
	Manerao mauri nace tale tale
	Gane gane o oha oha
	Prane prane o oha oha
	Surera surabhi bhare re

Surero Ei Jharjhar Jharna

Composer: Salil Chowdhury | Artist: Sabita Chowdhury

- Harmonica Notes
Maintained Originality
- by Riddhi Sanyal

Lesson 36: Surer Ei Jhar Jhar Jharna – Sheet Music with Harmonica Notes

8.7   Yeh Dosti Hum Nahi Todenge

This is one of the famous songs on friendship and from the famous movie Sholay. The duet from Kishore Kumar & Manna Dey gifted us this song with a different dimension.

About the song:

- *Song: Ye Dosti Hum Nahin Todenge*
- *Movie: Sholay (1975)*
- *Singer: Kishor Kumar, Manna Dey*
- *Lyrics: Anand Bakshi*
- *Composer: R D Burman*
- *Star Casts: Amitabh Bachchan, Dharmendra*
- *Music label: Universal Music India*
- *Taal: This song is based on 4/4 beats or Keherwa taal.*
- *Minor Notes: Nil*

Tempo: **Faster tempo** is chosen to depict the moving bike. The chosen tempo is 120 bpm or more.

Why chosen for Harmonica: Again needless to say it's the beauty of legendary music directory R. D. Burman to add Harmonica rhythms to express the happiness on a moving bike. The song has **Harmonica rhythms** during interlude music. So any newcomer in Harmonica loves to play this.

About the Notation: The notation of this was really hard to create as it contains lot of 1/4, 1/8 and 1/16 the beats. The key reason of breaking the notes into **quarter, eight and sixteenth**, is the Harmonica style beats. To play the song, we request you to listen to the song lot of times and then read the notations. The Harmonica beats are separately given for the easy of learning and facilitating so that the learner can generate more.

This above picture shows the snippet of the Harmonica beats. It's created with the simple rhythmic chords like C (C + E) together to blow, then Dm (D + F) together to draw and again C (E + G) together to blow. The beating pattern in this section (first measure) is like

- (1/8 + 1/16 + 1/16) ~ one 1/4 beat
- 1/8 + 1/8 ~ the next 1/4 beat
- (1/8 + 1/16 + 1/16) ~ one 1/4 beat
- 1/8 + 1/8 ~ the next 1/4 beat

This is a simulation of the actual beating pattern and don't think that it's 100% identical with the original. But it will lead you to similar beating pattern.

Once you can play this, you can experiment similar.

Only Antara 1 is given in the Staff Notes / Harmonica notes. Antara 2 also has similar tune & rhythm.

Lyrics:

Phrases	Lyrics
Bandish	Yeh Dosti Hum Nahin Todenge
	Todenge Dum Magar
	Tera Saath Naa Chhodenge
Antara 1	Are Meri Jeet, Teri Jeet, Teri Haar Meri Haar
	Sun Ae Mere Yaar
	Tera Gum Mera Gum, Meri Jaan Teri Jaan
	Aisa Apna Pyaar
	Jaan Pe Bhi Khelenge Tere Liye Le Lenge
	Sabse Dushmani
Antara 2	Logon Ko Aate Hain Do Nazar,
	Hum Magar, Dekho Do Nahin
	Are Ho Judaa Yaa Khafa
	Ae Khuda, Hai Dua Aisa Ho Nahin
	Khana Peena Saath Hai, Jeena Marna Saath Hai
	Saari Zindagi

What we will learn from this song:

- **Playing rhythmic song**
- **Simulating Harmonica chords in rhythm**
- **Playing note bending as needed**

Yeh Dosti Hum Nahi Todenge

Composer: R D Burman | Singer: Kishor Kumar, Manna Dey

- Harmonica Notes
Maintained Originality
- by Riddhi Sanyal

♩ = 120

Bandish

Ye - e do - s ti - i   hum na - hi - i to-de-n - ge-e-e   To - den-

| +6 | +6 | -5 | +4 | +4 | +3 | +3 | -7 | +7 | +7 | +6 | -5 | -5 | +6 | -5 | +4 | +6 | +6 |
| G | G | R | S | S | P | P | D | P | P | G | R | R | G | R | S | G | G |

To Coda

ge-e - e   dum ma - ga - r   Te - ra   saa - th naa   cho - den - ge

| -6 | +7 | -6 | -6 | +7 | -6 | +6 | -5 | -5 | -5 | +6 | +6 | +6 | -5 | +4 | +4 |
| m | P | m | m | P | m | G | R | R | R | G | G | G | R | S | S |

Musical rhythm in Harmonica

+6	-6	+7	+6	+7	+6	-6	+7	+6	+7	+6	-6	+7	+6	+7	+6	-5	+4
+4	-5	+6	+4	+6	+4	-5	+6	+4	+6	+4	-5	+6	+4	+6	G	R	S
G	m	P	G	P	G	m	P	G	P	G	m	P	G	P			
S	R	G	S	G	S	R	G	S	G	S	R	G	S	G			

Antara 1 (other Antara has same tune)

Me-ri jeet   te-ri jeet   te-ri haar   me-ri haar   Sun ye   me-e-ri jaan

| +7 | +7 | +7 | -7 | -7 | -7 | +7 | +7 | +7 | +8 | -7 | -7 | -7 | +7 | +7 | -6 | +7 | -6 | +6 |
| P | P | P | D | D | D | P | P | P | Ŝ | D | D | D | P | P | m | P | m | G |

Te-re gum   me-ra gum   me-ri jaan   te-ri jaan   Ai sa   aa-p-na pyar

| +7 | +7 | +7 | -7 | -7 | -7 | +7 | +7 | +7 | +8 | -7 | -7 | -7 | +7 | +7 | -6 | +7 | -6 | +6 | -7 |
| P | P | P | D | D | D | P | P | P | Ŝ | D | D | D | P | P | m | P | m | G | D |

Harmonica Rhythm

Jaan   se   bhi   khe-len-ge

| +6 | -6 | +7 | -6 | +6 | -5 | -5 | +7 | +7 | -5 | +7 | -5 | +7 | +7 | -5 | +7 |
| G | m | P | m | G | R | R | P | P | R | P | R | P | P | R | P |

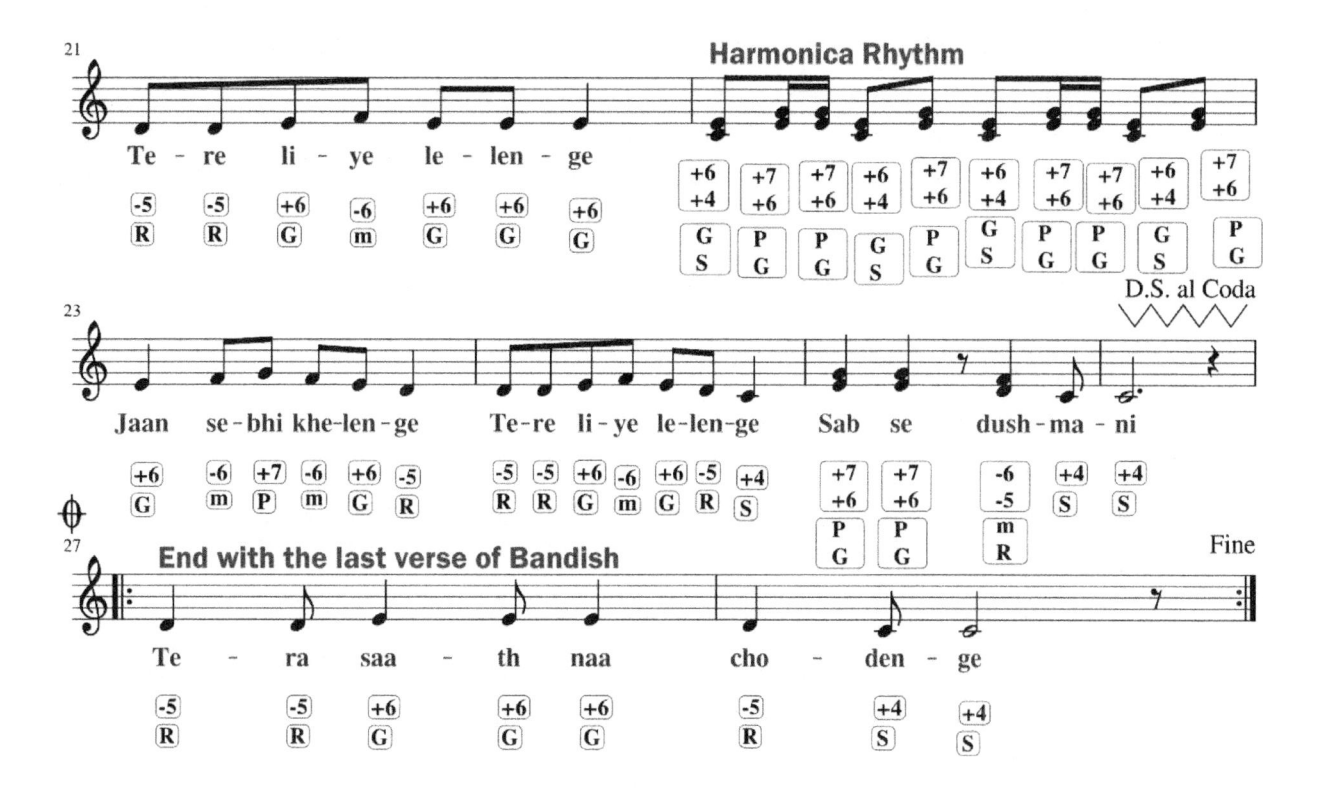

Lesson 37: Yeh Dosti Hum Nahin Todenge

8.8 Ajeeb Dastan Hai Yeh

This song is one of the romantic & country based in the Jazz rhythm. Our objective is to learn this particular pattern on music, especially the rhythm. That will help us to play similar songs.

About the Song:

- Song: Ajib Dastan Hai Yeh
- Film: Dil Apna Aur Preet Parai (1960)
- Singer: Lata Mangeshkar
- Music Director: Shankar Jaikishan
- Lyricist: Shailendra
- Star Cast: Meena Kumari, Raaj Kumar, J. Om Prakash, Nadira, Helen, Naaz
- Director: Kishore Sahu
- Taal: 4/4 Beat or Keherwa.
- Genre / Pattern: This song follows Jazz rhythmic pattern. The genre may be country.
- Tempo: Medium. For example, 120 BPM or slower is preferred.

Original Song: This song has been created with the influence from the English song "My Lips Are Sealed" by Jim Reeves which was released on 1956. That was 4 years before the release date of the song "Ajib Dastan Hai Yeh".

Learning from this song:

- Play & learn the Jazz Rhythm.
- Vibration will help to generate the feel.
- Interlude will help us to play end to end.
- Harmonize or play chords during Interlude or Actual song.

Lyrics:

Section	Lyrics
Bandish	Ajiib daastaan hai ye
	Kahaan shuruu kahaan khatam
	Ye manzilen hai kaun sii
	Na vo samajh sake na ham
Antara 1	(Ye roshanii ke saath kyon
	Dhuaan uthaa chiraag se) x 2
	Ye khwaab dekhatii huun main
	Ke jag padii huun khwaab se
Antara 2	(kisiikaa pyaar leke tum
	nayaa jahaan basaaoge) x 2
	ye shaam jab bhii aaegii
	tum hamako yaad aaoge
Antara 3	Mubaaraken tumhen ke tum
	kisiike nuur ho gae) x 2
	kisiike itane paas ho
	ke sabase duur ho gae

After every Antara, you have to return to Bandish as usual. Only the first *Antara* has been given with Notations. Rest of the *Antara* (s) are identical in tune.

Ajib Dastan Hai Yeh

Music Director: Shankar Jaikishan | Singer: Lata Mangeshkar

*- Harmonica Notes
Maintained Originality
- by Riddhi Sanyal*

Lesson 38: Ajib Dastan Hai Yeh

8.9   Salute to Covid Warriors – By Sri D. Madhusudan

This is one the finest music by Guruji Sri. D. Madhusudan to salute to the Covid-19 Warriors. Guruji has made this to practice the Dorian Mode (in Western). That is equivalent to the Kaafi Thaat. The Notes are following mostly Kaafi Raga and the composition is westernized. Guruji has prepared this Composition after the first Covid-19 Wave and this song is dedicated to Covid-19 Warriors. We remember when Guruji gifted this music to us for practice. That was during Covid situation and everyone was mentally down. This tune just simply purifies your mind and soul with the deep feeling when you salute the warriors.

About the Tune:

- **Name: Salute to Covid Warriors**
- **Composed By: D. Madhusudan**
- **Year of Publication: 2020 October**
- **Raga / Mode of Music: Raga Mishra Kaafi or Dorian Mode**
- **Tempo: Initially practice with medium tempo and finally prepare for fast one.**
- **Beats / Taal: It's based on 4/4 or Keherwa Taal.**

Minor Notes:

- **Komal Ga (Indian symbol g) or Eb w.r.t. C scale**
- **Komal Ni (Indian symbol n) or Bb w.r.t. C scale**
- **Tibra Ma (Indian symbol M) or F# w.r.t. C scale → this is used only once**

Few of the location, *Shudha* Ni or western note B is also used. That evolves or blends the *mishra bhaba* to Kaafi Raga.

Applicability to Harmonica: First of all, we need to practice this Dorian Mode in Harmonica to play lot of songs or to play any of the Raga belongs to Kaafi Thaat (Ex: Pilu, Bhimpalas, Kaafi, Shivaranjani, etc) and that has too many compositions in Bollywood songs as well as western. For example, the famous song by Bryan Adams – "Have You Ever Really Loved a Woman" is on Dorian Mode or Kaafi Thaat. Hindi famous Song "Roja Jaaneman" Song by A. R. Rahman and S. P. Balasubrahmanyam is on Raga Pilu & Desh. "Khilte Hain Gul Yahan" by Kishore Kumar is on Raga Bhimpalas and follows the Dorian Mode or Kaafi that. We can list 1000s of songs in that pattern of music and so learning this will help all musicians.

This particular tune by Guruji has nice rhythm too and so it's perfectly suites Harmonica to cover. Once you pickup this tune, you will learn –

- **Dorian Mode**
- **4/4 Fast Rhythm**
- **Starting a measure or section from off Beat**

Salute To Covid Warriors

Composer: Sri D. Madhusudan | Year of Publication: 2020 Oct

- Harmonica Notes
Maintained Originality
- by Riddhi Sanyal

♩ = 220

Bandish

+4	-5s	+7	-6	-5	-5s	+7	-5s	-5	-5s
S	g	P	m	R	g	P	g	R	g

Fine
To Coda

-6	-7	+8	-7s	-9	-9s	-9	+8	-8	+8
m	D	Ŝ	n	R̂	ḡ	R̂	Ŝ	N	Ŝ

+8	-7	-7s	+7	-7s	+7	-7	-6
Ŝ	D	n	P	n	P	D	m

D.S. al Coda

+7	-5s	-6	-5	-3s	+3s	-4	+4
P	g	m	R	ṉ	ḏ	Ṉ	S

Antara 1

+4	+7	-6	+7	+7	-6	+7	-5s	+7	-6	+7	+7
S	P	m	P	P	m	P	g	P	m	P	P

-5s	-7s	-7	-7s	-7s	-7	-7s	+7	-7s	-7	-7s	-7s
g	n	D	n	n	D	n	P	n	D	n	n

+7	+8	-8	+8	+8	-8	+8	+7	+8	-8	+8	+8
P	Ŝ	N	Ŝ	Ŝ	N	Ŝ	P	Ŝ	N	Ŝ	Ŝ

D.S. al Coda

+8	-9s	-9	-9s	-9	-7s	+7	-7	-6	-5	+7	-5s	-5	+4
Ŝ	ḡ	R̂	ḡ	R̂	n	P	D	m	R	P	g	R	S

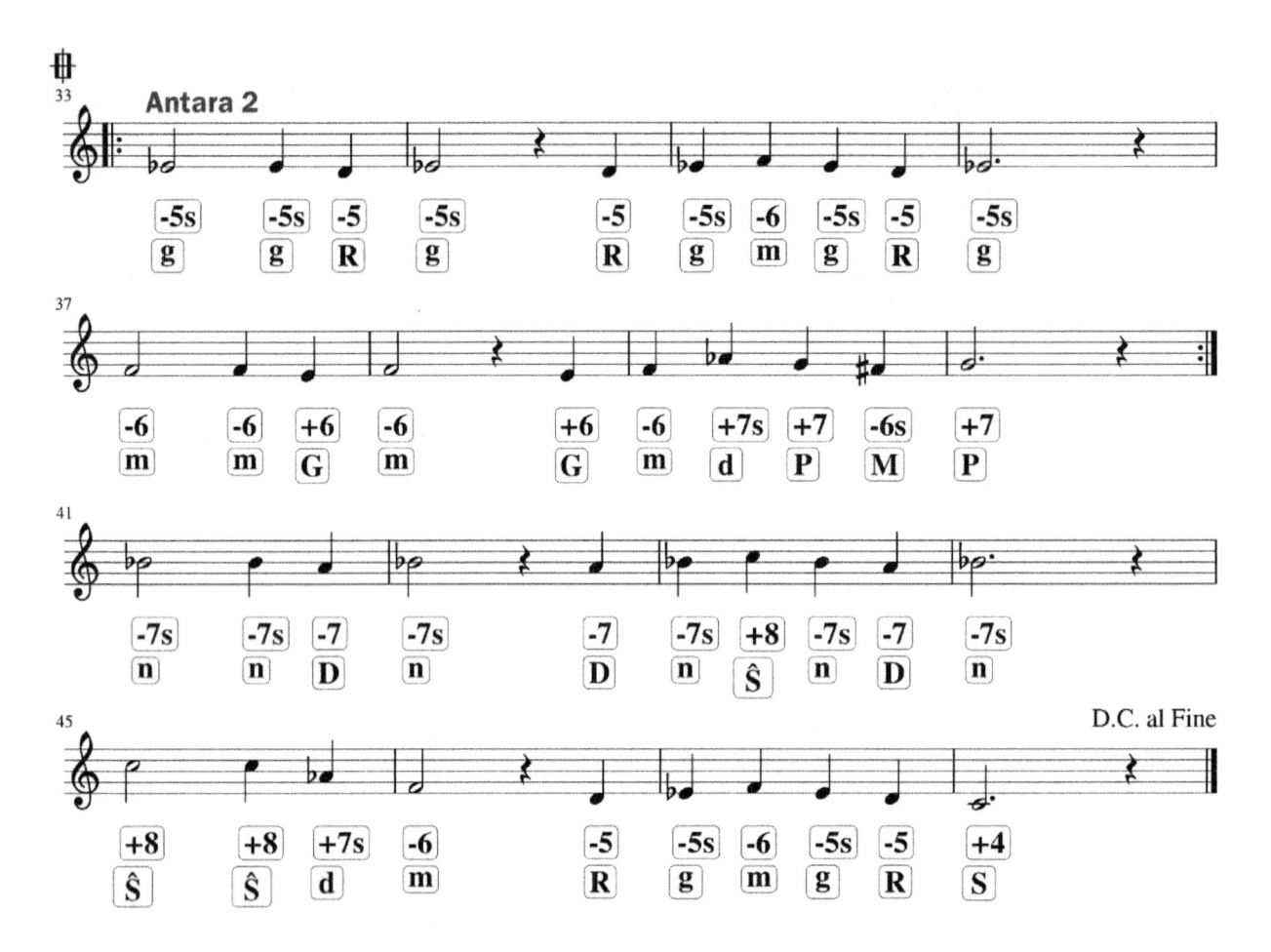

Lesson 39: Salute to Covid Warriors by D. Madhusudan

8.10 Mere Sapno Ki Rani Kab Aayegi Tu

This is one of the most popular romantic songs by Kishore Kumar. Needless to say any Harmonica player loves this song as the rhythm goes in Harmonica.

About the Song:

- Song Title: Mere Sapnon Ki Rani Kab Aayegi Tu
- Movie: Aradhana
- Year: 1969
- Singer: Kishore Kumar
- Lyrics: Anand Bakshi
- Music: S. D. Burman
- Music Label: Rajshri

Raga / Thaat / Pattern: **Follows the *Raga Bhairavi* according to Indian classical or Phrygian mode in western convention.** This song is the perfect blend of Indian Classical & western rhythmic chords.

Rhythm / Taal: This song follows **4/4 beat** rhythm or **Keherwa taal**. The rhythm depicts the sound of running train.

Why chosen for Harmonica: Well nothing much to say in this corner as S.D. Burman has introduced the classic train rhythm in Harmonica. Some of the musical sections, interludes, rhythmic chords are applied in the original song. Most harmonica learners in India love to play this song.

About creation of the notation: This song is on Bhairavi Raga (minor notes) and but the initial music section are on major notes. So it's really difficult to play the initial music + song notes in the same scaled Harmonica as there will be lot of scale changing. So to avoid the scale changing key of Harmonica, we have changed the original scale in E scale (making Ga as Sa). That will ease the notes for Harmonica on the song part. Only scale changing will be required to play the Initial / Interlude music parts. All of the *Antara* has similar notes and so only single *Antara* has been given with *Bandish*.

Pre-requisite to play this song:

- You need to practice the E minor scaled SARGAM (Phrygian mode). To simplify, play all major notes starting from Ga or E to higher Ga or higher E. like –
- G – m – P – D – N – Ŝ – R̂ – Ĝ
- GmP – mPD – PDN – DNŜ – NŜR̂ – ŜR̂Ĝ
- That will help you to concentrate on the scale E or Phrygian mode.
- This song demands fast rhythm as it's depicting the train sounds. You need to practice with Rhythm so that you can play starting from a beat or starting from off-beat.
- The starting music part of this song is on E major scale which turns out to be the opposite of the song which goes on E minor scale. So be sure, you understand and realize the differences. The

classic beauty of the composer is, how he blends the music on major notes and comes back to minor when the lyrics of the song goes on and that too with mixing of Harmonica, Guitar, Flute etc. So please listen to the original song for few times to be on the same page. As we change the song to play from E minor (no change key involved for harmonica), so to play E major in music, you have to do change key on Harmonica. We can't take both advantages 😊.

➢ Another way to play will be to collect couple of Chromatic Harmonica with scale C & scale E scales. With scale C, starting from Ga (E), you play the song. With scale E, you play the music in the interlude as it mostly on E major. But again, while coming back to the song from music, there will be few scale changing notes on E Harmonica too. So with all possibility, this song is one of the most challenging on Harmonica to cover entirely including music. Please try that option if you have the multiple harmonicas and give me a comment with hash tag **"#MouthOrganForEveryoneBook"** in Youtube or Facebook or Instagram.

What we will learn from this song:

- **Phrygian mode or *Bhairavi Raga* based music**
- **Play rhythmic chords in Harmonica (during the *Antara*)**
- **Start a section from Off Beat as well as normally**
- **Play faster rhythm like train sounds**

Section	Lyrics
Bandish	Mere sapnon ki rani kab aayegi tu Aayi rut mastaani kab aayegi tu Beeti jaaye zindagaani kab aayegi tu Chali aa, tu chali aa
Antara 1	(Pyaar ki galiyaan, baagon ki kaliyaan Sab rang raliyaan poochh rahi hain) x 2 Geet panghat pe kis din gaayegi tu
Antara 2	(Phool si khilke, paas aa dil ke Door se milke chain na aaye) x 2 Aur kab tak mujhe tadpaayegi tu
Antara 3	(Kya hai bharosa aashiq dil ka Aur kisi pe yeh aa jaaye) x 2 Aa gaya to bahut pachtaayegi tu
Ending	Chali aa, tu chali aa Chali aa, haan tu chali aa

Mere Sapno Ki Rani

Composer: S. D. Burman | Artist: Kishore Kumar

*- Simplified Harmonica Notes
Maintained Originality
- by Riddhi Sanyal*

2. Interlude Music Starts -->

33
| +7s | +7s | +7s | +7s | +7s | +7s | +7s | +7s | +7s | +7s | -8 | +10 | +10 | +10 | -9 | -8 | -7 |
| d | d | d | d | d | d | d | d | d | d | N | Ġ | Ġ | Ġ | Ř | N | D |

37
| -7 | -7 | -8 | -9 | -9 | -8 | -9 | -9 | -8 | -8 | -8 | -8 | -9 | +10 |
| D | D | N | Ř | Ř | N | Ř | Ř | N | N | N | N | Ř | Ġ |

41 **Interlude Music ends -->**
| +7s | +7s | +7s | +7s | +7s | +7s | +7s | +7s | +7s | +7s | +7s | -7 | -7 | -7 | -7 | -7 | -6 | +6 |
| d | d | d | d | d | d | d | d | d | d | d | D | D | D | D | D | m | G |

45 Antara 1 (Other Antara has same tune)

Harmonica Rhythm in the right section

Pya - r ki ga - li - yaan
| +6 | -6 | -7 | -6 | +6 | +6 |
| G | m | D | m | G | G |

+7	+7	+7	+7	+7	+7
+6	+6	+6	+6	+6	+6
P	P	P	P	P	P
G	G	G	G	G	G

49 Baa - gon ki ka - li - yaan
| +6 | -6 | -7 | -6 | +6 | +6 |
| G | m | D | m | G | G |

+7	+7	+7	+7	+7	+7
+6	+6	+6	+6	+6	+6
P	P	P	P	P	P
G	G	G	G	G	G

53 Sa - b ran - g ra - li - yaan
| -8 | -8 | -7 | -7 | +6 | +6 | -8 |
| N | N | D | D | G | G | N |

-9	-9	-9	-9	-9	-9
-8	-8	-8	-8	-8	-8
Ř	Ř	Ř	Ř	Ř	Ř
N	N	N	N	N	N

57 Poo - o - ch ra - hi hain
| +8 | -8 | +8 | -8 | -7 | -7 |
| Ŝ | N | Ŝ | N | D | D |

| -7 | -7 | -7 | -7 | -7 | -7 | -7 | -7 |
| D | D | D | D | D | D | D | D |

61 Pya - r ki ga - li - yaan Baa - gon ki ka - li - yaan
| +6 | -6 | -7 | -6 | +6 | +6 | +6 | -6 | -7 | -6 | +6 | +6 |
| G | m | D | m | G | G | G | m | D | m | G | G |

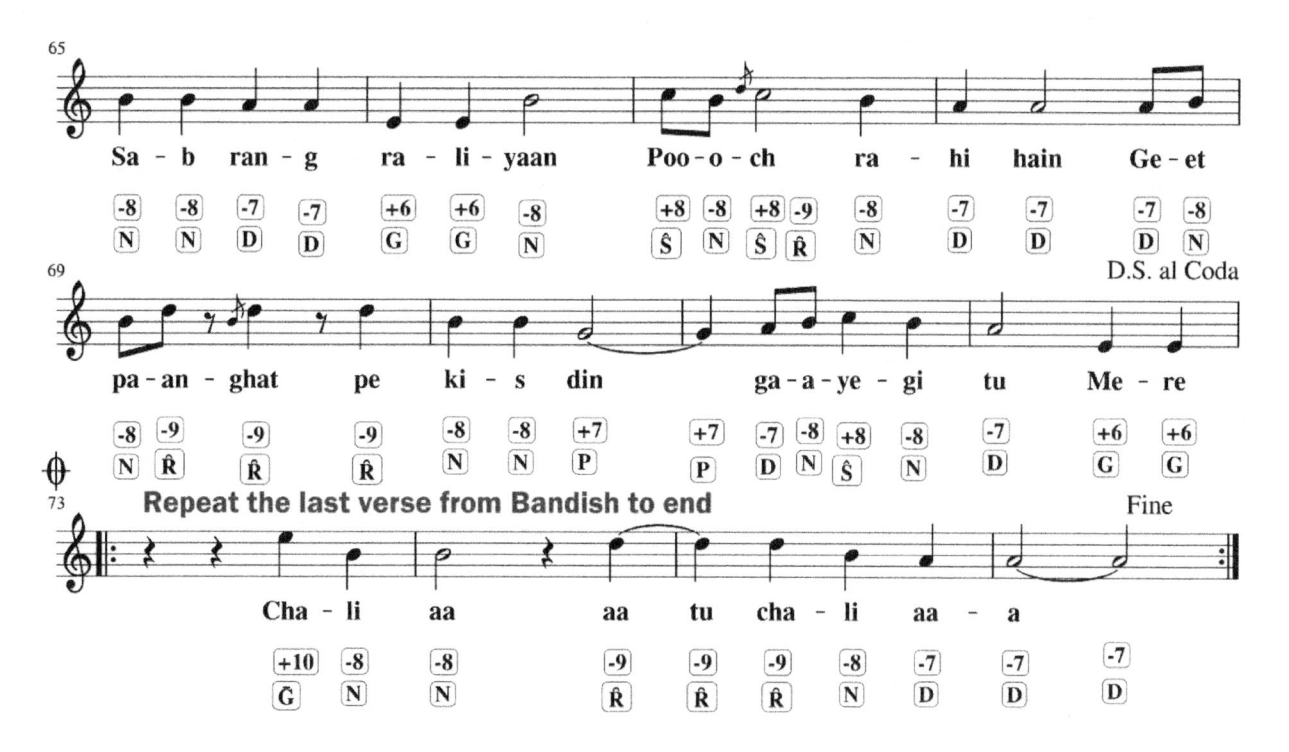

Lesson 40: Mere Sapno Ki Rani – Sheet Music with Harmonica Notes

### 8.11	Further Learning

Once you have completed all of the lessons, you can try out any songs from your own. We have listed some of the interesting songs which you may like to play. Some more guidelines are given to you to play or at least know the starting position to find the tune on your own.

➢ **Have You Ever Really Loved a Woman**

Song: "Have You Ever Really Loved a Woman?" by Bryan Adams, Released: 1995, Genre: Latin rock, Songwriter(s): Bryan Adams, Michael Kamen, Robert John "Mutt" Lange, Producer(s): Bryan Adams - Robert John "Mutt" Lange

You have already played a similar song in this advanced section which is in Dorian Mode or Kaafi Thaat. This particular song of Brian Adams, followes the similar where you have to play both Ga sounds – komal / minor ga (symbol g ~ D#/Eb) and normal Ga (symbol G ~ E). But this song has normal Ni sound and no minor there.

Beating patterns like 6/8. You can start this song like this –

Indian Notes:

"☐ S S | – – – | Rg RS – | – – – | Rg RS – | – – – | RS RS<u>N</u> – | – – –|"

"g – – | g – – | gmP mg – | – – – | gmP mg – | – – – | mg mgR – | – – –|"

"S R m | – – – | – – – | – – – | – – mG | RS – – |" ...

Western Notes:

"<u>G</u> C C | – – – | DEb DC – | – – – | DEb DC – | – – – | DC DC<u>B</u> – | – – –|"

"Eb – – | Eb – – | EbFG FEb – | – – – | EbFG FEb – | – – – | FEb FEbD – | – – –|"

"C D F | – – – | – – – | – – – | – – FE | DC – – |" ...

Rest of the notation you play and find out yourself.

➢ **Annie's Song (You Fill Up My Senses)" by John Denver.**

This is one of the nice melodies songs. This could be one of the best in Harmonica compared to other instruments. You can start from the higher Ŝ here like –

Indian Notes:

"– – Ŝ | Ŝ N D | Ŝ – – | N – – | D – – |"

Western Notes:

"– – Ĉ | Ĉ B A | Ĉ – – | B – – | A – – |"

This song has a nice romantic feel and you have to bring that with Vibration.

➢ **Baranday Roddur**

This by the Bangla Band **Bhoomi** in the album Jatra Shuru. This is one of the popular folk based fusion with very fast rhythm. You can start from

Indian Notes:

"P D Ŝ | – – – | – – – | P D Ŝ | – – – | – – – "

"P D Ŝ | Ŝ Ŝ Ŝ | Ŝ Ṙ ŜN – "...

Western Notes:

"G A Ĉ | – – – | – – – | G A Ĉ | – – – | – – – "

"G A Ĉ | Ĉ Ĉ Ĉ | Ĉ Ḋ ĈB – "...

You will need to play one minor note. You can find that yourself.

➢ **Kaisi Paheli Zindagani**

Well the Jazz / blues rhythm is one of the best mind-swinging one. We have plenty of Bollywood songs in that rhythm.

➢ **Ajeeb Daasta Hay Yeh** – detailed notation already given in this section.
➢ **Kaisi Paheli Zindagani** – by Sunidhi Chauhan, Movie: Parineeta, Composer: Shantanu Moitra
➢ **Aage Bhi Jaane Na Tu** – by Asha Bhosle, Movie: Waqt, Composer: Ravi
➢ **Zindagi Kaisi Hai Paheli** – By Manna Dey, Movie: Anand, composer: Salil Chowdhury

Assuming, you have already played the song "Ajeeb Daasta Hay Yeh" earlier in this section. Keep the rhythm continued and you can play either of these given songs. Here you need to play with little Bending style as these songs demands. The first line of "Kaisi Paheli Zindagani" is given below for quick pickup –

Indian Notes:

"ŜP – DNŜ ND | ŜP – DNŜ ND | m R – – | – – – – –"...

Western Notes:

"ĈG – ABĈ BA | ĈG – ABĈ BA | F D – – | – – – –"...

Find the notation yourself by playing and play at least 2 songs in a medley. That will be nice and innovative way to cover.

> **Hothon Se Chhoo Lo Tum**

Song Title: Hothon Se Chhoo Lo Tum, Movie: Prem Geet, Singer & Music Direction: Jagjit Singh, Music label: Shemaroo. This particular *Bhajan* is one of the best from Jagjit Singh. This can be performed on Harmonica nicely. This Bhajan is based out of Raga Yaman. So you have to play the Tibra Ma (symbol = M ~ F#). This is on slow 4/4 rhythm and has a great feel. You can start this song like this –

Indian Notes:

"– – – GR | GRS S SG RS | N̲ – – – |"

"N̲S SR RS G | R S – –"...

Western Notes:

"– – – ED | EDC C CE DC | B̲ – – – |"

"B̲C CD DC E | D C – –"...

You will love this *Bhajan* once you can pick and play.

"Don't limit a child to your own learning, for he was born in another time."

"The highest education is that which does not merely give us information but makes our life in harmony with all existence."

— Gurudev Rabindranath Tagore

9.0 Index, References & Appendix:

9.1 Index of Figures, Tables, Note Symbols & Lessons:

Figure 1: Author playing Harmonica in front of mirror to show the holding style 2
Figure 2: Diatonic Harmonica – Blues master from Suzuki on the Key Db / C# 10
Table 1: Diatonic Harmonica from Suzuki - Blowing Positions with Notes on the Key of C 11
Figure 3: The Chromatic Harmonica 11
Table 2: Chromatic Harmonica - Blowing Positions with Notes on the Key of C 12
Figure 4: Tremolo Harmonica from Easttop 13
Table 3: Tremolo Harmonica - East Asian Tuning - Blowing Positions with Notes on the Key of C 13
Table 4: Tremolo Harmonica – Asian Tuning – Blowing Positions with Notes on the Key of C 13
Figure 5: Holding Technique using Right Hand Thumb for Key changing 15
Figure 6: Holding Technique using Right Hand Index Finger for Key changing 16
Figure 7: The whistle style 16
Figure 8: The tongue assist style 17
Note Symbols 1: Octaves vs. all Notations 21
Note Symbols 2: Notation Conventions – All Possible Notes in 12 Hole Harmonica 23
– Staff Note vs. Harmonica Tabs vs. Indian Notes 23
Note Symbols 3: Notation Conventions – Mostly Played Major Notes 24
– Staff Note vs. Harmonica Tabs vs. Indian Notes 24
Note Symbols 4: Every Good Boy Does Fine – Learning Treble Clef 25
Note Symbols 5: Key Signature 25
Note Symbols 6: Time Signature 4/4 – Keherwa Taal 25
Note Symbols 7: Time Signature 3/4 – Dadra Taal 26
Note Symbols 8: Measures 26
Note Symbols 9: Note Symbols & Gaps 26
Note Symbols 10: The Tempo 27
Note Symbols 11: Dotted Notes 27
Note Symbols 12: Measure is repeated 28
Note Symbols 13: Verse is repeated 28
Note Symbols 14: Repeat and jump to another section 29
Table 5: Play middle octave (western notes) 30
Table 6: Play middle octave (Indian notes) 30
Lesson 1: Play Middle Octave 31
Lesson 2: Add Lower & Higher Octave Notes with Middle Octave & Play in 4/4 31
Lesson 3: Play 2 Same Notes at a time 33
Lesson 4: Play 2 Sequential Notes at a time 34
Lesson 5: Play Alternative Notes 35
Lesson 6: Play quarter & eighth Notes in 4/4 beats Rhythm 36
Lesson 7: Play Progression on 3 Notes in 6 beats (3/4) 37
Lesson 8: Play Progression on 4 Notes in 8 beats (4/4) 38
Lesson 9: Learn Rest / Gap for Whole, Half, Quarter and Eighth Gaps 39
Lesson 10: Play Quarter & Eighth Notes & Rests (4/4) 40

Table 7: Simple Tunes for Beginners & summary on the learning 43
Lesson 11: Play 'Twinkle Twinkle' 44
Lesson 12: The Wheels on the Bus 46
Lesson 13: Play Happy Birthday 47
Lesson 14: Row Row Row your Boat at C and C# 50
Lesson 15: Old MacDonald Had a Farm 52
Lesson 16: Play 'We Shall Overcome' 54
Lesson 17: Jingle Bells 56
Lesson 18: Do-A-Deer / Do-Re-Mi 58
Lesson 19: Sholay Harmonica Tune 59
Lesson 20: Simple Tune in Deshkar 62
Table 8: Intermediate Level Tunes & summary on the learning 66
Lesson 21: A Chal Ke Tujhe 69
Lesson 22: Santa Lucia 71
Lesson 23: Jamaica Farewell 73
Lesson 24: Title Music – A Happy tune by D. Madhusudan 76
Lesson 25: O Sona Byang – a Salil Chowdhury Song 77
Lesson 26: Hai Aapna Dil 81
Lesson 27: Minuet 82
Lesson 28: Pran Chay Chokkhu Na Chay – A Rhythmic Tagore Song 85
Lesson 29: Five Hundred Miles 87
Lesson 30: Music for Wind – Waltz rhythm 90
Table 9: Advanced Level Tunes & summary on the learning 95
Lesson 31: Can You Feel the Love Tonight – The Lion King Song 98
Lesson 32: March Music by D. Madhusudan – March rhythm 101
Lesson 33: Chala Jata Hoon – Sheet Music with Harmonica Notes 105
Lesson 34: Indian Folk Song - Tomay Hrid Majhare Rakhbo 108
Lesson 35: Waltz 12 by D. Madhusudan – Waltz rhythm 112
Lesson 36: Surer Ei Jhar Jhar Jharna – Sheet Music with Harmonica Notes 115
Lesson 37: Yeh Dosti Hum Nahin Todenge 119
Lesson 38: Ajib Dastan Hai Yeh 123
Lesson 39: Salute to Covid Warriors by D. Madhusudan 126
Lesson 40: Mere Sapno Ki Rani – Sheet Music with Harmonica Notes 131

9.2   References

This book has the reference of various Harmonicas product details or links. As well as, we have used lot of songs with the lyrics to prepare the lessons. The references of lyrics of the songs are also listed below. All of these external links were referred on or before Dec 2022. This book has no connection towards those external links. If some link is not available or changed, then you can search them from the product name or song name.

i. Tremolo Harmonica retrieved from https://en.wikipedia.org/wiki/Tremolo_harmonica as on Dec 2022.

ii.	Tremolo Harmonica image retrieved from Easttop "East top Tremolo Harmonica Key of C, 24 Holes Tremolo Mouth Organ Musical Instrument for adults and Professionals with Silver Cover T2403" https://www.amazon.in/dp/B01GZN8IMC/
iii.	Tower Mouth Organ Harmonica 24 Holes Key-C With Scale Change Option, Silver - https://www.amazon.in/dp/B00QGDYE20
iv.	JUAREZ 24 Holes JRH24CHBL Harmonica Brass Reed Plate Aluminium Cover Chromatic Tower Mouth Organ With case Blue https://www.amazon.in/dp/B08JW1N3KC/
v.	Easttop 10 Hole Chromatic Harmonica - retrieved from https://www.amazon.in/Easttop-T10-40-Mouth-Organ-Harmonica/
vi.	Swan Chromatic Harmonica 12 hole - retrieved from https://www.amazon.in/Swan-Hole-Chromatic-Harmonica-SW1248/dp/B00P7ESYU2
vii.	Hohner Chromatic Harmonica - retrieved from https://www.amazon.in/dp/B00LE6JFGY
viii.	Suzuki Chromatic Harmonica - retrieved from https://www.amazon.in/dp/B00133A19S
ix.	Reading Sheet Music retrieved from https://www.wikihow.com/Read-Piano-Sheet-Music
x.	Notation Symbols retrieved from https://en.wikipedia.org/wiki/List_of_musical_symbols
xi.	Dotted Note retrieved from https://en.wikipedia.org/wiki/Dotted_note
xii.	Repeats can be retrieved from https://en.wikipedia.org/wiki/Repeat_sign
xiii.	Da Capo Repeats can be referred from https://en.wikipedia.org/wiki/Da_capo
xiv.	Dorian Mode retrieved from https://en.wikipedia.org/wiki/Dorian_mode
xv.	Kaafi Thaat retrieved from https://en.wikipedia.org/wiki/Kafi_(thaat)
xvi.	Kaafi Raga retrieved from https://en.wikipedia.org/wiki/Kafi
xvii.	The Lyrics of the song "We Shall Overcome" is retrieved from https://en.wikisource.org/wiki/We_Shall_Overcome_(song)
xviii.	The overview of the song "We Shall Overcome" is retrieved from https://en.wikipedia.org/wiki/We_Shall_Overcome
xix.	The overview and lyrics of "Jingle Bells" have been retrieved from https://en.wikipedia.org/wiki/Jingle_Bells
xx.	The tune and songs of the movie Sholay have been retrieved from https://en.wikipedia.org/wiki/Sholay and https://www.imdb.com/title/tt0073707/
xxi.	The overview of the song "Silent Night Holy Night" is retrieved from https://en.wikipedia.org/wiki/Silent_Night
xxii.	Lyrics & overview of Ode To Joy - retrieved from: https://en.wikipedia.org/wiki/Symphony_No._9_(Beethoven)
xxiii.	Overview of the song "Lakdi Ki Kaathi" has been retrieved from https://en.wikipedia.org/wiki/Masoom_(1983_film)
xxiv.	The overview of the song "Jesus loves the Little Children" has been retrieved from https://en.wikipedia.org/wiki/Christian_child%27s_prayer#Jesus_Loves_the_Little_Children
xxv.	Overview of the song Imagine by John Lennon is retrieved from https://en.wikipedia.org/wiki/Imagine_(John_Lennon_song)
xxvi.	Overview and lyrics of the song "A Chal Ke Tujhe" have been retrieved from https://hindilyrics123.com/aa-chal-ke-tujhe-lyrics-in-hindi-10030.html
xxvii.	Overview and lyrics of the song "Santa Lucia" have been retrieved from https://en.wikipedia.org/wiki/Santa_Lucia_(song)
xxviii.	Overview and lyrics of the song "Jamaica Farewell" by Harry Belafonte have been retrieved from https://genius.com/Harry-belafonte-jamaica-farewell-lyrics
xxix.	The overview of the song "O Sona Byang O Kola Byang" and it's lyrics have been retrieved from https://www.firedekha.com/2020/08/o-sona-bang-o-kola-bang-lyrics.html
xxx.	The overview & Lyrics of the song "Hai Aapna Dil" have been retrieved from https://www.lyricsindia.net/songs/2250
xxxi.	Lyrics & overview of Minuets have been retrieved from: https://en.wikipedia.org/wiki/Minuets_in_G_major_and_G_minor
xxxii.	The overview and lyrics of the song "Pran Chay Chokkhu Na Chay" have been retrieved from https://www.geetabitan.com/lyrics/P/pran-chaay-chokshu-na-chaay-lyric.html
xxxiii.	Lyrics & overview of 500 Miles have been retrieved from https://en.wikipedia.org/wiki/500_Miles
xxxiv.	The overview of the song "Bachelor Boy" is retrieved from https://en.wikipedia.org/wiki/Bachelor_Boy
xxxv.	The overview of the song "Galyat sankali sonya chi, Hi pori kona chi" is retrieved from https://www.lyricsmash.com/galyan-sakli-sonyachi-lyrics-english-translation/
xxxvi.	The Overview of Titanic Song "My Heart will Go On" is retrieved from https://en.wikipedia.org/wiki/My_Heart_Will_Go_On
xxxvii.	The Overview of the song "Phoolon Ke Rang Se" is retrieved from https://en.wikipedia.org/wiki/Prem_Pujari
xxxviii.	The Overview of the song "Gazab Ka Hai Din" is retrieved from https://en.wikipedia.org/wiki/Qayamat_Se_Qayamat_Tak

xxxix.	The overview and lyrics of the song "Can You Feel the Love Tonight" have been retrieved from https://genius.com/Walt-disney-records-can-you-feel-the-love-tonight-lyrics
xl.	The overview and lyrics of the song "Chala Jata Hoon" have been retrieved from https://www.lyricsindia.net/songs/2058
xli.	The overview and lyrics of the song "Tomay Hrid Majhare Rakhbo" have been retrieved from https://www.gdn8.com/2018/03/tomay-hrid-majhare-rakhbo-lyrics-folk-song.html
xlii.	The overview and lyrics of the song "Surero Ei Jhor Jhor Jhorna" have been retrieved from https://lyricsbengali.in/lyrics/surer-ei-jhor-jhor-jhorna-lyrics
xliii.	The overview and lyrics of the song "Yeh Dosti Hum Nahi Todenge" have been retrieved from https://www.lyricsindia.net/songs/2614
xliv.	Overview and lyrics of the song "Ajeeb Dastan Hai Yeh" have been retrieved from https://www.hinditracks.in/ajeeb-dastan-hai-yeh-lyrics
xlv.	Overview and lyrics of the song "Mere Sapnon Ki Rani" have been retrieved from https://www.hinditracks.in/mere-sapnon-ki-rani-lyrics
xlvi.	The overview of the Song "Have You Ever Really Loved a Woman?" is retrieved from https://en.wikipedia.org/wiki/Have_You_Ever_Really_Loved_a_Woman%3F
xlvii.	The Overview of Annie's Song (You Fill Up My Senses)" by John Denver is retrieved from https://en.wikipedia.org/wiki/Annie%27s_Song
xlviii.	Overview of the song "Baranday Roddur" is retrieved from https://www.gdn8.com/2010/04/baranday-roddur-song-lyrics.html
xlix.	Overview of the song "Kaisi Paheli Zindagani" is retrieved from https://en.wikipedia.org/wiki/Parineeta_(2005_film)
l.	Overview of the song "Hothon Se Chhoo Lo Tum" is retrieved from https://www.hinditracks.in/hothon-se-chhoo-lo-tum-jagjit-sing

9.3   Appendix

Topic	Details & Corresponding Western equivalent w.r.t scale C
Swar	Swar (Swara) is the Sanskrit / Hindi term of single Note.
Swaralipi	Swaralipi is the Sanskrit / Hindi term of Notation.
SARGAM	In Brief, combination of SRGmPDNŚ are called Sargam. It's the small musical piece combination of the notes. Ex: SG RS Gm PN Ś NŚ NP mG RS
Shuddha	The 7 major notes SRGmPDN are termed as Shuddha Swars. Corresponding western notes are CDEFGAB
Komal (Flat) &Tibra (Sharp) notes	There are 4 Komal Swars / notes – Komal re, symbol r (C# / Db), Komal ga, symbol g (D# / Eb) Komal dha, symbol d (G# / Ab), Komal ni, symbol n (A# / Bb) There is only 1 Tibra Swar –Tibra Ma, symbol M (F# / Gb)
Higher Octave Symbols	Ŝ, ř, Ř, ḡ, Ḡ, ḿ, Ḿ, Ṕ, ḋ, Ḋ, ṅ, Ṅ, Š
Middle Octave Symbols	S r R g G m M P d D n N
Lower Octave Symbols	Ṣ, ṛ, Ṛ, g̣, G̣, ṃ, Ṃ, ? d̩, Ḍ, ṇ, Ṇ
Indian Taal & it's Bol	A bol is a mnemonic syllable. It is used in Indian music to define the taal, or rhythmic pattern, and is one of the most important parts of Indian rhythm. Bol is derived from the Hindi word bolna, which means "to speak."

Rabindra Sangeet	Rabindra Sangeet, also known as Tagore Songs, are songs from the Indian subcontinent written and composed by the Bengali polymath, Greatest Poet, Rabindranath Tagore, winner of the 1913 Nobel Prize in Literature. Tagore was a prolific composer with around 2,230 songs to his credit. The songs have distinctive characteristics in the music of Bengal, popular in India and Bangladesh.
Sthayi / Bandish / Gat & Antara	Bandish or Gat (also called Sthayi) is the first two lines of the Song or Raga with the Taal. The next section or verse is called Antara. These texts can be observed in the Lesson Notes to illustrate the section of the verse.
Talim	The initial lessons which Guru teaches to a student.
Drut Laya	Laya is the speed or tempo in Indian languages. Drut means faster. So faster tempo. Ex: more than 140 bpm
Madhya Laya	Madhya means medium. So medium tempo. Ex: 120 bpm
Vilambit Laya	Slower tempo or less than 100 bpm.
Raga Names Used	We have used plenty of Raga references such as Kafi, Bhimpalas, Pilu, Shivaranjani, Deshkar, Yaman, Bhupali, Bhairavi etc. Explaining Raga is outside the limits of the book. You can check the particular Raga in Wikipedia https://en.wikipedia.org or Tararang site. Ex: Raga Bhairavi - https://www.tanarang.com/english/bhairavi_eng.htm
Baul	This is the genre of Folk Music from north east India and especially from Bengal. Baul is also referred to the group of people who live by singing or playing the Baul songs. It's a form of *Sadhana* or spiritual practice to offer the songs to God.

10.0 About The Author

Riddhi has been in the music industry for more than 22 years. Apart from **Harmonica**, he plays **Flute, Piano, Guitar, Ukulele, Melodica, Sarod, Mandolin & Tabla**. His mother, *Smt. Gargi Sanyal* is a well-known *Rabindra Sangeet* singer and learnt from Legendary *Suchitra Mitra* at Rabithirtha. Grandmother, *Smt Tripti Saraswati* was a classical singer and had taken coaching to *Pt. Jamini Ganguly* and Legendary *Sri Manabendra Mukherjee*. Sister, *Smt Madhupa Sanyal* (student of *Pt. Ajay Chakraborty* at Shrutinandan). Musical gathering (*Ganer Ashor*) is very much common at home and sometimes everyone is deeply tuned into music, that even time passes from evening to late night on those homely musical occasions.

During childhood, Riddhi has learned Tabla from famous teacher **Sri Abhijit Barhouri** at Malda. During those days, famous singer & Harmonium maestro, **Sri Alok Bhadhury**, used to come at our home at teach music. During this time Riddhi has learned **Harmonica** by practicing the Bollywood Songs, Tagore Songs on Harmonica. During his college life, Riddhi has started to learn Flute from his friend **Sri Sajal Banerjee**. Later on Riddhi has learned to play the Bamboo flute by self-practicing and performed in the college functions.

During staying at USA (2007 – 2010), studying at various library at Minneapolis, he has learnt sheet music. He has performed at US, at the **Minneapolis during Durga Puja festival** organized by BAM. There he has played *Rabindra Sangeet* and North Eastern *Bhatiali* Music. Everyone has appreciated with the type of music and especially on Larger Flute (F#) they have first time observed at US. Feedback he received after function - "*It's rare to have Indian flute / Bansuri in the US functions and it was awesome to listen to the Indian & North Eastern tunes*". His wife Priyanka had accompanied on that function with Keyboard.

Finally, he has made with musical Guruji, **Sri D. Madhusudan** at Jadavpur class during 2010. Since then it is all Guruji's guidance. Riddhi has performed classical music, Raga, Light classical music, Rabindra Sangeet, Bollywood Golden Era songs, Patriotic songs etc. on Flute & Harmonica in lot of places - During Durga Puja, Diwali & Maa Kali Puja at Kolkata, Uttarpara, Malda, Dasaswamedh Ghat, Varanasi, Function at Bangalore, Mangalore, etc.

By profession, Riddhi is Sr. Architect in one of the largest Software Company. Staying in IT industry for 20 years, he has never stopped practicing or teaching music. He has performed in front of several customer visits and corporate functions. Once he had played Raga Hansadhwani on Flute to the CIO & Board of directors of one large Company. His eyes were perplexed and he was like overwhelmed during the entire duration of concert. At the end, he told that, until now he has listened to this kind of concert in TV. First time he has seen someone playing in front of him and he has no words to explain the sensation.

Riddhi has started **coaching on Flute and Harmonica** since last 7 – 8 years. Post Covid days, he has started online classes. Interested learners may contact him on WhatsApp or Facebook for further learning.

11.0 Other Publications from the Author

Book	Link	Description	Scan to View & Listen
	**Flute For Everyone** https://www.amazon.in/dp/B07Y8DL1K3	Learn the basics of Flute (Bansuri) in 60 days and play **prelims, Bollywood Songs, World Music,** and slowly enter into **Indian Classical Music.**	
	**Mouth Organ for Everyone** https://www.amazon.in/dp/B0BSB2X9WH	Complete Guidelines to learn Harmonica from **Basics to Advanced level.** Lessons are in Staff Notes + **Harmonica Holes** + Indian Notes. Video included for Beginner lessons.	
	**Tagore Songs Collection in Sheet Music – Volume One** https://www.amazon.in/dp/1649832435	**10 Beginner Level** Tagore Songs are published in Staff Notes for the Piano, Guitar, Ukulele, Flute, Harmonica and all **C Scaled Instruments.**	
	**Tagore Songs Collection in Sheet Music – Volume Two** https://www.amazon.in/dp/1639408851	**10 Intermediate Level** Tagore Songs are published in Staff Notes for the Piano, Guitar, Ukulele, Flute, Harmonica and all **C Scaled Instruments.** Also Available in Color Print in Amazon US & Worldwide.	
	**Violin Notation for Tagore Songs** (Volume One) https://www.amazon.in/dp/1685546358	5 Beginner and 5 Intermediate level **songs published** for Violin, Mandolin, Piano, Guitar & any **D Scaled** Instruments.	
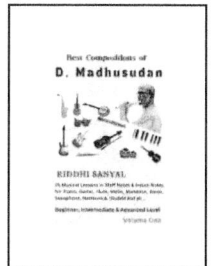	**Best Compositions of D. Madhusudan – Volume One** https://www.amazon.in/dp/B0CHQNNG5J (Scale C)	Total 25 Notations across Beginner, Intermediate, **Advanced & Expert** level tunes are published in Sheet music & Indian Notes. **Musicians can learn & improve their skills on any stroke / bowing instruments like** Piano, Guitar, Ukulele, Flute, Harmonica, Saxophone etc.	

12.0 Feedback & Contacts

This book is designed in such a way that, readers across the world will be able to learn Harmonica. The book covers all levels of learners – **Beginners**, **Intermediate** and **Advanced**. Even if someone is learning this book without any knowledge of music, he or she can quickly pickup the **techniques, notes, rhythms** on Harmonica. The book follows unique way of 3 notation system – **Staff Notes, Harmonica Tabs** and **Indian Notes**. For making this simplest, only the treble section of staff notes has been illustrated. Biggest advantage of this book is it contains around **40 exercises in 3 notations** and with key learning from each of these notes. Interested learners can pick the further learning sections and can learn to play **additional 15 songs**. Ultimate objective is to learn various patterns of music in Harmonica and play independently. **You can share your review & rating. Upon your feedback, next version can be improvised and re-published. Even you can tag your Audio / Video recording with hash tag "#MouthOrganForEveryoneBook"** in any social media so that hard work of book can be illustrated.

Author Page: https://www.amazon.com/author/riddhi (you can get all published books here in this link)

Email: Riddhi.Sanyal@gmail.com

Whatsapp Number: +91 9051653871

YouTube Channel: https://www.youtube.com/c/MusicalJourneys
(Please subscribe to support and get new updates)

Facebook Page: https://www.facebook.com/mu.instr

Instagram: https://www.instagram.com/riddhi.sanyal/

Printed in Dunstable, United Kingdom